Vegas
Rag Doll

Vegas Rag Doll

A True Story of Terror and Survival
as the Wife of a Mob Hitman

Joe Schoenmann
and Wendy Mazaros

Stephens Press • Las Vegas, Nevada

Certain names in this book have been changed and are reflected by pseudonyms.

Designer: Sue Campbell

Library of Congress Cataloging-in-Publication data
Schoenmann, Joe. Mazaros, Wendy.
Vegas rag doll : a true story of terror and survival as a mob hitman's wife / Joe Schoenmann and Wendy Mazaros.
220 p. : photos ; 23 cm.
ISBN-13: 978-1-935043-33-1 Hardcover Edition
ISBN-13: 978-1-935043-56-0
ISBN-13: 978-1-935043-34-8 e-Book Edition
Wendy Hanley Mazaros's story of sex, drugs, corruption, and murder, features many well-known figures from Las Vegas's history, in addition to her life as the wife of Tom Hanley, a hitman for the mob.
1. Mazaros, Wendy. 2. Hanley, Tom. 3. Organized crime—Nevada—Las Vegas. I. Title. II. Mazaros, Wendy.

364.1'092 [B]   dc22   2011   2011920370

STEPHENS PRESS, LLC
A Stephens Media Company

P.O. Box 1600 (89125-1600)
1111 West Bonanza Road
Las Vegas, Nevada 89106
www.stephenspress.com

Printed in the United States of America

CHAPTER ONE

Wendy only knew the body in the freezer as "Old Joe." She had no idea when it got there or its name when it had been alive. Had it been a wrinkled old man or young and athletic? Tom never unlocked the door. All she knew was that Old Joe's arms and legs must have been sawed or broken like a fryer chicken to fit, because the olive-drab icebox only looked big enough to house a frozen teenager.

Tom Hanley, Wendy's husband, had great fun with the stashed body, tying it to his poor stab at humor about the weather, a Las Vegas obsession. "I bet Old Joe doesn't mind 115 degrees," he'd chuckle, or "Funny Old Joe can sleep in that cold right through the day."

"Old Joe" disappeared into the background as all household objects do, and more so at the Hanleys' Ogden Avenue home, which was always filled with a dark white noise, a cacophony of snickering over misdirected police investigations into Tom's latest murder, or how-to instructions on tossing a body down an abandoned mine shaft and the interesting sounds it makes bouncing off ledges and rock outcroppings on the way down. Even the backslapping glee at the sight of gems and gold and silver dumped onto the living room floor after an arranged jewelry store heist just became part of the family din, the background noise easily tuned out.

Tom and Gramby, Tom's son from his first marriage, stood by the freezer now, hunched over a table covered with unrolled blueprints. Gramby had just emerged from the bathroom, rubbing the fresh needle puncture on his arm. He rarely smiled except at times like these, full of chemical orgasmic bliss. But when he did smile, Wendy saw Warren Beatty.

They talked of where to place the bomb at the Alpine Village this time, since the authorities had found and de-activated the bomb they'd placed there in September.

"We get on the roof and put it deeper into the ventila-tion, where it can't be seen—and no one else knows a thing," Tom said. "We don't tell anyone."

"Anyone" meant Al Bramlet, boss of the Culinary Union, the most powerful labor organization in Nevada. Bramlet paid the father-son team well to help restaurants and taverns understand the social good—and self-preserving quality—of a unionized work force. The Culinary boys had been picketing Alpine Village every day for decades. Bramlet was tired of their refusal to give in, so he put Tom and Gramby to work.

Wendy leaned against the doorjamb, taking it all in with hooded eyes, twisting her hair with one finger, a slight pout that awakened dimples and made her even prettier in feigned petulance, a look she thought would grant the excuse needed to stand and listen to their secret plans.

She'd been there five minutes when father and son stopped cold.

For a second, the two just drank her in. Every man wanted a girl like Wendy. She weighed maybe one hundred pounds, each parsed in symmetric perfection throughout her five-foot-four frame. Long brown hair crashed and curled at her shoulders before dropping farther down her back. Fine facial features accentuated her brow, cheeks or lips—details men noticed after curves and dips drew them in—so she never wore heavy makeup. Petulant but confident, too, another look perfected in the terror of family life based on intolerance for weakness.

She looked back at them, brow lifted, really looking more through than at them. The disinterest of this young beauty, feigned or genuine, threw them, kept them quiet a few beats more in wonder of the thought behind that perfect face.

Gramby despised her, but heroin sanded away his hard edges, dulled the baser emotions, helped him see the world in the soft glow of a Vaselined camera lens. Heroin also ruled his life. Police had found him passed out in the yard of a friend's house one night, nearly dead of an overdose. Stern warnings from the authorities or from his dad—if they only know how the drug made him feel, they'd laugh with him at their words.

Heroin opened his heart, ironed out the wrinkles, spanned the lightless fissures in memory, and let him reminisce, his words flowing ice-cream soft about the first brawl Tom employed him to cause at a union rally, his first flawless killing, dad's patience in teaching him how to wire a bomb.

"Tell her about the JFK job," he asked his dad.

Tom shot him a look.

"Dad was a part of that hit," he said, looking at his dad with a slight smile and pure admiration. "He was one of the shooters, something to do with Castro and the unions. There were real reasons Kennedy was killed."

"Shut up, Gramby," Tom said.

"Why? It's true. You should be proud."

Tom pulled a pistol from his waist.

"I said shut up."

"If you can't tell her, then why do you even let her sit here and listen?"

"You little son of a—"

Gramby flew out the front door with Tom on his tail. Even high on drugs, Gramby was light years faster as he sprinted around the corner to his house, two hundred feet away. Tom gave up after a few steps outside, walked back in, and sighed. Tom looked taller than his six feet. His shadow engulfed Wendy. He walked into a room and people felt his presence, a darkness that made them straighten up and step out of his way. He didn't mind showing his scalp—only the insane would mention it—white as a bone with a downy stand of white hair starting about mid-scalp and down the back of his head.

He gazed hard at Wendy, scanning for the slightest weakness, the merest twinge of distress. Not a wrinkle on that pretty face. Her arms hung like will-o'-the-wisps. She had as much interest in their spat or JFK as a cop had writing a parking ticket.

If Tom had taken part in the presidential murder, it wasn't mentioned in the massive investigation culminating in the Warren Commission report. While the FBI interviewed more than ten people in the Las Vegas area, including casino mogul Jackie Gaughan, the interviews focused more on waiters, bellmen, pit bosses, and other bit players who may have seen Jack Ruby, the man who killed Kennedy's assassin, Lee Harvey Oswald. Benny Binion got brief mention by the Warren Commission. Gaughan told investigators he had talked to Binion about Ruby, asking Binion if he had remembered seeing Ruby in Vegas. Neither had. That seemed to satisfy the Feds.

Wendy had turned eight the September before Kennedy's assassination, and Gramby's comment brought her back to that day in third grade. Her teacher cried openly in front of the class. At home, Mom sat at the kitchen table looking at the black-and-white photo of her standing next to the president at the Nevada Test Site.

Now, some twelve years later, on a virtually unknown street in downtown Las Vegas, in a house with a freezer she believed held a dead man, a father and son were acting out a macabre, Ozzie and Harriet-esque dispute about an integral chapter in the country's history. Wendy was only nineteen years old but already wondered how life had dumped her here, in this place, with these killers.

Tom disappeared into the bedroom. Alone in the quiet, she could pretend. The drab white of the walls, the guns throughout the house, the locked freezer, and the voices of the dead whispering in Tom's ear would find their way into her nightmares one day.

When it was quiet like this, Wendy could make believe it was all normal. Sure, there was food in the refrigerator and she had friends, even if they were Tom's friends, bewhiskered cronies who'd engaged in union battles at his side. These guys were in their forties before she was even born. Not that she could complain, seeing as how she had chosen to marry a man thirty-eight years her senior.

Hanging out with friends her age was out of the question. Tom wouldn't have it. She could see the justification in that. "He just wants me to be safe," she'd think. And God knew twentysomethings in the 1970s, with the way they were experimenting with drugs and protesting against the government and sleeping around, well, it really *wasn't* safe to be out with them. The one time she took the car to a friend's house, she walked outside a bit later to find the car missing. Walking back into her friend's house, Tom showed up a minute later, entered the house, and dragged her to his car. He and Gramby had been sitting at the end of the block watching the whole time she was there.

Tom loved her. She knew that much. And he had reason to be protective. Las Vegas was a tiny city. She never told him but she's certain he knew. Somehow. About her attempted suicide, her rape by a boyfriend at fifteen. Then raped again two years later by a poker player and his roommate. Then the months she spent enslaved in a roadside Texas motel-turned-brothel where she was forced to meet the demands of oil workers and cattlemen who smelled of lube grease and rancid sweat, men who grunted with workmanlike indifference as they fucked her.

Her truth? The thirty-eight-year difference meant nothing. Tom was her savior, a graying white knight. He didn't kill just anyone. It was with purpose. Did he kill Kennedy, or even go to Dallas as part of a team to "take care of" the president? Why the hell should she care? Dallas was thousands of miles and years away in a state she hated after her experience there. Here and now, Tom was at her side. He was her protector and maybe the only reason no one from her checkered young life had tried to kill her.

At his side, people were nicer to her, more deferential. Teddy Binion again started to treat her like the queen of the casino, the way he did before he sent her to Texas, before he asked his "stringy-haired little girl" to show his gamblers a good time.

Hell, even mob enforcer Tony Spilotro crawled and begged forgiveness—sure, with the muzzle of Tom's pistol against the back of his head—after joking that Wendy looked like Tom's daughter.

But that honor belonged to the little girl growing inside of her. Wendy touched the perfectly round bulge in her abdomen and smiled. This was proof of some thread of goodness, if only because Wendy was creating something so innocent, so perfect, so untouched.

Wendy walked into the bedroom at the front of the house.

Then she got back to work, unhooking the black suits hanging in the closet and laying them gently on the couch. The clothes still reeked of woodsy cologne, cigarette smoke, and Al Dreyer, a lawyer who had lived with Tom until he died on the operating table at a local hospital. Or, as Tom put it, until he ordered the surgeon to botch the surgery.

Tom and Al were close friends. Had been for years. Dreyer was Tom's personal lawyer, and Tom let Dreyer live in his house for free. And, on occasion, Tom let Al, who had ruined his career with alcohol, have a taste of his beloved whiskey. Problem was, Dreyer knew too much, Tom had said, including that he had aided Tom in a murder. Now what, Tom thought out loud, would a drunk like Al do if some cop offered him all the whiskey he could handle if he spilled his guts?

So Al disappeared.

That had happened years earlier. And now Tom wanted Al's stuff out of the house. As Wendy put away Al's clothes, she replaced them with Tom's suits and slacks. This was happy work befitting her vision of how real families worked together. The happy housewife keeping the house in order while her husband earned a living.

Wendy rummaged through the pockets of each shirt, pair

of pants or suit coat, removing money or screws, bullet casings or bits of wire and anything else dropped in there from Tom's day job as an air conditioner repairman and his night job killing people or blowing up union-resistant businesses.

Then she found a note.

Mary Lou Hanley, Tom's first wife, wrote it.

She died in her bed in January 1975. The official story goes that Tom found her dead in her bed. Her county death certificate blamed her death on cirrhosis and alcoholism.

But the note that Wendy found, signed by Mary Lou, hinted at something else. Mary Lou disgusted herself, the note said, and she feared she disgusted her husband, and was sick and tired of a life ruled by alcohol. "Tom, I cannot go on living within this hell. The house is empty since Al passed. I'm disgusted with my life. Mary Lou."

Wendy read and reread the folded pink stationery. What the hell is this? she thought. Did Mary Lou kill herself? If she did, why did Tom keep this note in the pocket of a coat he still wore?

She felt a tinge of anger. Not jealousy. How could she be jealous of a dead woman? But if Tom pined for his dead wife, why did Wendy have to constantly do his bidding, never stray from his sight, never have friends of her own? Tom and Mary Lou had been married for about forty years, but he had told Wendy their love had died many years earlier. So why did he keep holding onto this note? She's dead, for chrissakes.

"Tom," she yelled. "Tom, come here. I found something."

He walked into the room, tall and big and brimming with animal ownership, the sense of never being caught off guard, of knowing how to handle every situation.

"What is it?"

"What's this?" she held out the note.

Her voice was flat, without inflection. Anger threatened Tom, too. Unchecked, anger can blind people and lead them to do and say stupid things. Anger would get Wendy killed.

She said nothing as he read it. He breathed in deep, tightened his lips.

"Sit down," he said. "Please." He was so gentle that Wendy's eyes welled with tears.

He started from the beginning, the point at which he first met Mary Lou. Her very sight swelled his heart. They moved to Las Vegas, a place in dire need of any person trained in a skilled trade. That need allowed someone with his mechanical acumen to make a life for his wife, and eventually for five children.

Hanley became head of the union of sheet metal workers. Three decades later, he called Las Vegas' most powerful people his best friends. He had even been asked by those same powers to run for governor (a murder charge killed that ambition).

All the while, he and Mary Lou felt strong together, true and supportive. Then the unthinkable happened. They had a young son who became very sick. A doctor gave him a shot of penicillin to battle an infection. They didn't know he was allergic to penicillin. He went into shock and died within minutes

Parents don't outlive their children. It's not supposed to happen. When children die, parents often break up. Their little boy's death shattered Tom and Mary Lou, but they stayed together. Tom worked harder. Mary Lou diluted the pain with drink. Soberness meant her little boy's smiles came into focus, meant she could feel the absence of his tight hugs and his tiny breath on her neck as she held him. She drank vodka, so much of it that when she sweated, it came out her pores.

Tom took her to medical doctors and psychologists and counselors and friends, even preachers. She drank straight through doses of Antabuse, a prescription drug that makes the user violently ill when ingesting alcohol.

Tom had no choice. He put the word out to all the bars and stores to never sell or serve alcohol to his wife. He kept a close eye on her and locked up the liquor at home. He locked up perfumes and colognes, anything containing alcohol.

When Tom came home from work, there'd be Mary Lou waiting for him with a shot glass in hand. They'd exchange pleasantries, then Tom would go about his nightly routine reading the paper, watching TV. All the while, Mary Lou followed and stood behind him, her trembling hands squeezing tight the shot glass. That small, thick-walled glass was her chalice, sanctified by a gnawing need, an itch behind her eyes, a craving that hurt her joints, the ague from an ever-present flu.

She paused where he paused. Looked where he looked.

Then he'd unlock the cabinet and grab the vodka.

"Goddamn drunk," he'd say as he poured a few shots.

Wendy heard and wanted to cry, but held silent.

Tom said he tired of what Mary Lou had become. So one day, he made her a deal. He'd let her drink as much vodka as she wanted, but she had to write the suicide note and take a sleeping pill between each swig.

One drink. One pill. One drink. One pill.

More than an hour and a bottle of vodka later, she lay perfectly still, her eyes shut forever.

"She finally looked at peace," Tom said. He didn't know what to do with himself, having never told anyone else the story. He shrugged. Didn't know what else to say or what to touch or how to move.

"Oh Tom," Wendy buried her head in his chest. She felt weak. Her hands and feet tingled as blood in self-protection drained from her extremities. Blotches of blackness began to fill her sight but she held still, steadied herself and fought off passing out. She looked down at the gun tucked into Tom's waistband.

"My little Winnerferd," he whispered.

They hugged for a minute more. Then he stood up, pulled out his gun, and slapped it on top of the writing desk. He opened the top drawer and pulled out a pen and a clean sheet of typing paper. He pulled back the chair for her to sit at the desk.

"What's this for?" she asked.

"Just write what I say." His voice was gentle and sad and vulnerable. She knew what he was asking her to do.

Giving her time to write each word, he recited the sad life story that led Wendy to kill herself. Tormented by her brother's criminal troubles stemming from an alcoholic father who beat him without mercy, the memories were too unforgettable, too much to bear. She felt unworthy of life.

Wendy faltered and hesitated for just a moment, but long enough to aggravate Tom. She jumped when he slammed his gun on the table. Then she wrote on.

The pen shook in her hand until she took a deep breath and let it out slowly. She choked back tears. She could show no fear, not a hint of upset. She couldn't let her "suicide" become a reality, to become another victim of Tom's killing machine.

"I love my Winnerferd very much," he said.

"I love you, too, Tom."

She signed her name. He folded and put the note in his shirt pocket. He stood behind her, stroking her hair, rubbing her shoulders.

"You know I'll never have to use this, right?" he said. "All this is is insurance, nothing more."

"I know, honey," she said

He slammed his gun on the desk, looped her brown hair behind one ear, then leaned over close to whisper.

"Just remember," he said, forming a gun with his hand and putting the index finger to her temple. "Silence is the fence around wisdom."

CHAPTER TWO

Kids lead normal lives in Las Vegas, too. In the early '70s, Wendy's school district was considered one of the top five in the country. In the '50s and '60s, the city was so small that her parents not only knew their neighbors, they even talked to them. Las Vegas police officers knew strangers by sight simply because they recognized everyone who lived there.

Residents dressed Midwest or Northwest conservative because so many had moved to the dry, hot desert to escape the cold winters or endless rain and drizzle. For women, it was lengthy printed skirts or unfaded worker's jeans. Blue collar defined the men, many of whom sank roots while working at Nellis Air Force Base. Others were second generation, the sons and daughters of Hoover Dam workers.

Before Wendy was born, her parents, John and Patricia Watson, had both been transferred to Las Vegas while in the Navy. John got out of the military and co-owned a trucking company, Associated Moving and Storage. Patricia worked for high-level military officers at the Nevada Test Site. That's what Wendy figured anyway, because her mom had a high-level security clearance but never talked about what she did, just that she oversaw an entire department. But it was all top secret and important enough that she took home about twice as much money as John.

Even by the standards of the rest of the country, which

held Las Vegas in the same regard as another planet, the Watsons had a normal American life.

Not every American, however, earned mention by Walter Cronkite on the nightly news, as John Watson did in 1965. Cronkite, the man who held the country's collective soul in the palm of his hand ever since his stoic news persona broke while announcing the death of John F. Kennedy. He stopped talking, choking up a bit, wiped an eye, and forever endeared himself to the masses.

In June of that year, just before Wendy turned nine, Sears and Roebuck hired John Watson's company to transport between four hundred and five hundred pieces of art— paintings, lithographs, and engravings—from the Sahara Hotel and Casino to a warehouse in Los Angeles. The works had been collected for the company by actor and art collector Vincent Price and included Salvador Dali's "Mystical Rose Madonna." Watson drove one of three vans for the five-hour drive, and all three left the Sahara parking lot at ten a.m. on Tuesday, heading south down Las Vegas Boulevard, the only route out of town. By nightfall, only two vans had made it to the warehouse.

Neither of them was driven by Watson.

Cell phones didn't exist. Or pagers. There was no way to get a hold of him, and Watson didn't call in from a pay phone. By Wednesday morning, Las Vegas and Los Angeles police joined in the search. Price told reporters, "I'm worried."

Around six p.m. on Wednesday, long after his fellow drivers had arrived at the warehouse, police found Watson's van parked in front of a tavern in Alhambra, a suburb about fifty miles from his destination. Watson was blind to the hour. He had spent the last two days measuring time in beer cans and had lost count. Police arrested him but charges were never filed.

Cronkite delivered news of the artwork's recovery with a smile, saying simply that the delivery driver had "made a few too many pit stops."

It didn't take long after that fiasco for Watson's partner to force him out of the business. Never one to let reality stand in his way, Watson immediately started a new company called Las Vegas Transfer and Storage.

And he kept drinking.

Patricia Watson, by comparison, was a saint. Her work at the Nevada Test Site kept the family afloat. That stability came at a price. Patricia's steady work—requiring a two-hour drive to and from the Test Site each day—also meant she wasn't home when the kids woke up, and she saw them for only a few minutes before they went to bed.

John Watson was dad and mom for most of the time the kids were awake and at home. That wasn't often, though. He stayed home only two days a week, the rest of the time spent trucking around the Southwest. That left the kids to fend for themselves mostly. Wendy and her older brother, Michael, took risks that a watchful parent would never allow.

Such as sitting behind the car of the Hoover vacuum cleaner salesman making a cold call on the Watson home in 1958.

After closing the deal and selling John Watson the new Hoover Convertible vacuum cleaner, a new model that became the company's best seller for many years, the salesman jumped into his car and backed up on his way to the next home on his list. He hit the brakes after he heard the screams.

The impact snapped Wendy's collar bone, gave her a concussion, and she spent the rest of that scorching Mojave Desert summer with casts on one leg and one arm.

Less than a year later, Wendy's sister, the oldest of seven kids, was carrying a heavy cast-iron skillet full of hot grease in the kitchen. The pan twisted Phyllis's wrist, spilling the still-crackling bacon grease onto Wendy, who was milling at her feet. With third-degree burns over half her body, Wendy's sisters put her into a cold bath, then ran next door. The neighbors took her to the hospital. Her mom took rare time off from work to stay at her side until she was released. The burns left redness on her young, pliable skin that disappeared over time.

In first grade, while playing outside the house, Wendy peeked into her older sister's window. From outside, rooms look taller, somewhat faded, less real. The room of her sister, then about fifteen, was stuck somewhere between child and young woman. The walls were adorned with sheets of notebook paper that her sister had decorated with bulbous hearts that encircled the names of herself and the new boy she loved that month.

Teddy bears on shelves smiled down at her bed, which was covered by a pink woolen blanket. On top of the pink blanket laid her sister on her back. John Watson was on top of her.

Still in his clothes, resting his weight on his elbows, he looked down into his daughter's face. Wendy watched her sister scrunch up her face and turn away. Dad whispered into her ear. Wendy ran away.

A month later, that sister ran away with a member of the Gents motorcycle gang. They lived together in North Las Vegas. She was pregnant at sixteen. Decades later, her sister stared ahead toward their dad's coffin and said quietly to her dad, to her sisters: "I sacrificed my life for you, my younger sisters."

John Watson never explained why he did it. Guilt? A sense of injustice? The mood swings of an alcoholic? In any case, it didn't matter to his son, Michael. Michael only knew that when he caught that look in Dad's eye, it meant he was in danger.

If any kid deserved a beating, John Watson might have surmised, it was Michael. Always fidgeting. Always getting into things. Goddamned kid needed discipline. Little son of a bitch needed to know there were consequences. If the kid wouldn't listen to a scolding (and he never did), John's fists would do the teaching.

It became so common, especially since Patricia didn't get home until late, that Michael learned how to show no fear. He'd tell Wendy he couldn't feel anything behind his arms and legs. "Nothing hurts me," he'd say. Defiance fed John Watson's beatings. When Michael screamed, Wendy and her younger sister, Caroline, would run to their beds and press pillows against their ears.

Psychologists could have a field day analyzing Michael's behavior, given the fact that he started lighting fires when he was seven. He burglarized his first home at eight.

Wendy cried at the sound of every beating. With only thirteen months between them, Michael was her best friend. They shared secrets and spent hour upon hour in their playground, the desert. The two would spend hours after school looking for lizards, digging caves. Living not too far from Nellis Air Force Base, they unearthed plenty of bullet casings. Sometimes they'd find something they had never seen before, such as rigid fins on a heavy oval made of metal. The thing was too heavy to throw, but if they put their weight behind one foot, they could shove it down the road. Then it became a fun game, shoving the thing back and forth to each other in the street.

That's when the fire department showed up.

"It's live," they told John Watson, who was rubbing his eyes as if from a sleep. They showed him the metallic oval with fins. "If the tip had hit just right, it could have blown up half the block."

It made the papers.

Michael paid for it.

And just once, John Watson paid for it, too. In the middle of a beating one night, Patricia came home early from the Test Site. She heard Michael crying, heard the heavy thuds from his bedroom. Instinct took over. She kicked off a high-heeled shoe, ran at her husband, and tried with all her might to drive the heel deep into his skull. Blood streaming down his face and back, John Watson begged her to stop.

She did. He did, too, at least for the night.

❖ ❖ ❖

From the peak of Mount Charleston or a tiny window in the growing number of tourist-filled planes flying into town, it was hard to imagine screams in that quaint little desert town. In 1960, just as Wendy reached age five, the desert still owned most of the Las Vegas Valley. The city held all of 64,405 souls, about double the number living in the rest of the county. Desert tortoises and tarantulas kept far from the relatively mild lights of the infant Strip, but still had plenty of room to roam.

Las Vegas was an oversized Mayberry. In the quiet neigh-borhoods, everyone's business was everyone else's. The casinos, though, were a different story. Employees and customers held fast to the secrets that filled the hotel rooms and gambling pits. It's good for business. All of which made the Watson kids something of an anomaly and an occasional business distraction.

After all, it isn't all that often that a barkeep and his bleary-eyed denizens see little kids, with sleep in their eyes, wandering into a bar at midnight. The kids thought it was weird, too. Half asleep, they weren't sure what was going on when Patricia Watson rousted them from sleep, put them in the car, and drove from bar to bar looking for her husband and his beloved can of Schlitz.

Taverns in Las Vegas aren't unlike taverns anywhere else. Schlitz, Bud, PBR. Bar-top slots are unusual the first time you see them, then they become as expected and indispensable as bar stools. At night, Vegas bars are different, though, because they become the watering holes for the casino girls just getting off work. Cherry-red lipsticks, butt-cheek high or higher mini-skirts, layered hair swirled like meringue piled high and sprayed stiff with a dangle over the eye, they were adorned to become the figments of future dreams and return visits. Many, too, had kids at home Michael and Wendy's age. Self-reflection can be deadly to a tavern's bottom line.

Word in Mayberry spreads like wildfire. Not that there's anything a tightly knit community can do simply because one wife with children in tow is spotted a few times scouring downtown taverns looking for one man. But people take note. Neighbors hear the cars and rustle of kids late at night.

So one night in the summer of 1959, John Watson left the house when Patricia Watson was out of town on business. The neighbors saw John leaving and made a phone call. Within minutes, social service employees and police swarmed the Watson house and took the children to a shelter. Wendy, almost three, Michael and Caroline were allowed to stay together in one foster home. Wendy's memory of the house forever killed her taste for oatmeal and raisins, because that's all she remembers being fed.

It took two months, but Patricia Watson got them all back. Assembled in the living room at home, she sat them down and looked each of them in the eye, her own welling with tears. John sat at the kitchen table in the other room reading a newspaper.

"We will never be apart again," she swore. "All we have in life is each other."

The black-and-white naiveté of childhood is fleeting, but Mom's ease and calm reinforced whatever tiny slice of Beaver Cleaver normality existed in the Watson household. She never touched alcohol. Not a drop. When she talked to the kids, it was as if the words came from the mouth of God. Not the Old Testament God of wrath and destruction. But a God of respect, love, protecting, and understanding.

The Watson family's personality changed when she merely stepped through the door. Wendy and the other kids felt safe with her around. She listened and smiled. They all wanted her attention, all wanted just to be touched by her, just to touch her themselves.

Patricia Watson's integrity and reliability were the reasons she kept her job working for top administrators and generals at the Nevada Test site and Area 51 for almost thirty years. She made them feel like everything would be all right, too.

Not that the family knew exactly what she did or for

whom she did it. The kids knew her work took her to a top-secret base some eighty miles northwest of Las Vegas— Groom Lake, or, as popular culture has dubbed it, Area 51—and a short distance from the Test Site, where the military detonated 950 nuclear bombs between 1951 and 1992.

At the very least, it was an interesting place to hold the annual Test Site employee picnic. Every spring, Patricia Watson took the kids to meet other Test Site parents and kids. For all the times that Armageddon was played out under its desert skin, outsiders conjured images of the Test Site as a hell on earth. Its nuclear-spawned craters dug so deep they would keep their conical shape forever. The Test Site landscape looked like nothing else on Earth.

And Michael and Wendy loved it. They ate their fill of hamburgers and hot dogs and egg salad. And they explored the alien land. Beyond a few patches of jade-green fauna, the Mojave Desert appears no place for life, let alone play. Brown is the dominant hue, breathtaking heat its sustenance. But even here, amid the contours of mountains that appear sharp enough to cut diamond, there is beauty. The lone mesquite tilted and craning for even more sun in the middle of a wash, impossibly tiny flowers fluorescing after a spring downpour, the quiet of a church deep in the desert amid wild mustangs.

Man-made beauty here, too.

The last of some two hundred above-ground detonations of nuclear bombs, most of them set off at the Nevada Test Site, happened in 1962. By then, Wendy had seen plenty of mushroom clouds. Her mom would let the kids know ahead of time when a test would happen so they wouldn't be scared when the earth shook. Wendy and

Michael would run into the desert, perch themselves atop a hill, and watch the cloud billow into the sky sixty-five miles to the northwest.

The Test Site produced other wonders, too. Michael and Wendy found something new at the first employee picnic held there in 1965, two years after legislation passed to stop above-ground detonations. The two were used to seeing scorpions and black widow spiders. Even residents who never ventured into the desert knew of scorpions; they infested homes, a stomach-turning fact made apparent when the lights were off and a scorpion's tiny body glowed in the rays of an ultraviolet light.

The Test Site scorpion of 1965, however, was different. Wendy and Michael found it behind one of the buildings they played behind as their elders talked and ate baked beans and grilled burgers. As big as a palm rat and as green as Midwestern grass, this scorpion acted like a city rat at the sight of the two kids: It went about its business as if they weren't even there. Michael poked it with a stick. It didn't back away. It turned to square off against him and tiptoed his way, the stinger over its head jabbing at the stick Michael held in his hand.

Wendy screamed and ran around the building to her mom.

"Michael's fighting a giant scorpion!"

Within minutes, two men wearing lead-lined suits showed up. One caught the scorpion with long metal tongs and dropped it into a cage held by the other.

Patricia Watson remained calm, like always, as Wendy and Michael peppered her with questions. "Radiation from years of tests," she told them, "had the power to alter an animal's appearance. That's what happened with the scorpion. The two men in the lead suits were going to study it to find ways to make sure it doesn't happen to people."

❖ ❖ ❖

Years later—a year or so after Tom had died—Wendy and her mom were driving home from the Meadows Mall. Patricia, looking out the passenger-side window of the car, said something that made Wendy remember that great green scorpion.

"I want to tell you something, Wendy. There are beings out there looking after us." Wendy was certain Patricia was trying to offer some kind of comfort.

"You mean like God, like angels?" Wendy asked.

Patricia shook her head. She had seen her daughter indicted for murder, watched as she pleaded guilty to conspiracy to commit murder, and only recently begun to unravel bits and pieces of the horrors her daughter had witnessed while married to a killer. She wanted to offer a degree of comfort she hadn't been able to provide during Wendy's years with Tom.

"No, not God."

"Don't tell me—aliens!" and Wendy started to laugh.

"I mean other beings. They are real and they are here and they are watching over us," she said. "That's all I'm going to say."

Two weeks later in March 1979, Patricia Watson died of a brain aneurysm. John Watson had died years earlier.

CHAPTER THREE

At thirteen, Michael had become one of the Las Vegas Police Department's "usual suspects" whenever they got a call about some petty downtown crime and desert fires. Police visits to the Watson home became so frequent that Patricia Watson learned the sound of their tires on asphalt, recognized the sound of their shutting car doors. She hid Michael when she had time and told the police he was out playing.

Forced by the embarrassment that came with each police visit—they'd see the neighbors turn off their lights so they could peer through the curtains without being seen—and the thought that separating Michael from the negative influences of Las Vegas might keep him out of trouble, the Watsons moved again. This time, it was a ranch house five miles south of Fremont Street near McCarran Field, which by 1966 handled more than one million visitors annually. It was a favorite place to play. Michael and Wendy dared each other to lie at the end of a runway while prop-planes careened toward the landing strip, seemingly just beyond their grasp.

Wendy began to smile more.

In 1966, as the U.S military started sending troops to Vietnam, John Watson bought Wendy a bit of freedom. In a sign that the family's finances had begun to stabilize, he bought Red, a thirteen-year-old horse retired from a life sprinting for gamblers at Santa Anita Race Track. Her little sister, Caroline, got a horse, too.

It might not have happened had his wife not tried to punch holes in his skull with her shoe. After the troubles with Michael, and the sheer realization that his wife hated his guts, John had a rare moment of clarity and stopped drinking.

He even showed sympathy for Michael. Michael, who had been in therapy and on potent experimental drugs since he was seven, awoke screaming in the middle of the night from nightmares. Ritalin, a decades-old drug just being introduced to children, might stop the fidgeting, might create a façade of calm and focus. But whatever was tamped down during the day came out at night.

Wendy was always the first to run to his bed. Then Mom. Sometimes even Dad.

❖ ❖ ❖

The isolation of the desert gave Wendy all the time she needed to be with the love of her young life, Red.

Red, who let her steer him wherever she wished, who cared not a whit that she ran him hard, who shared the same joy at disappearing deep into the quiet of the desert. Her best friend, Emily, had a horse, too. She'd ride over and together the two would race to newly built Caesars Palace. They'd tie up their horses, leaving them to drink from the fountain, and go into the casino where Emily's dad oversaw the valet service and would treat them to lunch.

Not far from Caesars, along what is now Sunset Road, stars and locals would mingle at the Rocking Horse Ranch. Wendy and Emily would trot around the ranch on their horses, until enough people gathered outside on the fence to watch and make bets. Then, taking off their shoes and saddles to be as light as possible, the two would race each other to whoops and hollers, with the winner usually getting a small cache of money from the bettors.

The tourists, townies, starlets, and casino bosses didn't whoop it up simply for the thrill of the race. As Wendy entered her teens, she was growing into an uncommon beauty. In Wendy, tourists and entertainers used to leggy showgirls sensed a refreshing innocence, a farm-fresh purity. They had no idea nor wanted to know about her home life. They shared in the glee this pretty little girl had with her horse, a perfect counter to endured nights of gambling and smoking and women. When Wendy would erupt in her joyful laugh, immediate and true and as unstoppable as a hiccup, that freedom drew them even closer.

Red gave her hours of time away from thoughts of Michael. Her brother, now fifteen, was in and out of juvenile hall. Sentenced to a boot camp in the mountains west of Las Vegas, he returned claiming he had been raped by a counselor. He ran away and was found several hours later with frostbite on his feet so bad he was taken to a hospital.

In and out of "juvie," Michael hardened. John Watson never tried to hit him again after Michael one night fought back and bloodied his dad's nose. He was troubled, but he was still Wendy's brother and there's no bond stronger than the one forged out of the pains and glories of family. Even as they grew into their teens, they hung out together, sneaking out of the house at night to shoot pool in North Las Vegas.

They grew closer when Wendy had to give up Red.

As the Watsons' family wealth grew, they finally bought their own house in an upscale subdivision of Charleston Heights, near the municipal golf course and not too far from Lorenzi Park. Moving was a moment of immense pride for Wendy, now at the age where the realization of status and its symbols of conveyance—homes and clothes and friends—start to crystallize. Having moved at least ten times since birth, she would now live in one place. Not just any place. Not a used house. It was new and in one of the nicest parts of Las Vegas.

But moving also meant Wendy had to lose Red. You can't have a horse in the middle of the city's newest development. Emily said she'd take the horse, care for it, and let Wendy ride him whenever she wanted. Wendy kissed Red goodbye and for two weeks cried herself to sleep. Childhood had passed.

Michael took advantage of the loss. With his buddies, and Wendy the only girl, they became a loosely organized gang that typically snuck out at night to shoot pool in North Las Vegas.

One time they became burglars. On the way to the store, they shortened the route by hopping a fence. Suddenly, Michael veered into a storage shed, pulled out a hatchet, and started swinging it into the home's back door. When he had a hole big enough for his arm, he reached in and unlocked the door. Wendy followed him in, begging him to stop. He laughed it off and dashed into the kitchen, where he filled bags with groceries before fleeing. No sirens. No police. They got away with it and walked down the middle of the dimly lit neighborhood street laughing and taking bites of whatever food they had taken.

The only other time Michael broke into a home, he almost got Wendy and his girlfriend shot. Michael was dating one of her friends. The three were driving around when he jerked the car to a stop.

"Just be a minute," he said. The two girls had no idea what he was up to.

He got out, jumped a fence, ran to a garage window, and climbed in. The girls heard nothing for a minute. Then came a crash, followed by Michael flying out the front door of the house. Behind him was a man with a handgun.

Michael got in the car, squealed out, with the home-owner behind firing his pistol. Halfway down the street, Michael did a U-turn and pointed the car at the man standing in the middle of the street pointing the gun at the car.

Wendy and her friend got down, terrified as a few bullets hit the car. At the last second, the man jumped aside and Michael, laughing, sped down the road.

"Did you see that?" Michael said. "Just like in the movies!"

"Michael, we almost got killed!" Wendy said.

"Oh, quit being a mom. It's over. We're fine."

Michael was all smiles, with an arm around the waist of Wendy's friend. It was the first time in months Wendy had seen him so alive. All in all, they were unscathed, she thought. He was her best friend, too. She calmed herself. She pushed away the terror and soaked in her brother's glee.

Home late that night, she lay in bed and waited, but no one knocked on the door, no red lights, no sirens. It was fine, just like Michael said.

John Watson, though, started taking notice. He didn't know Wendy and Michael were sneaking out at night. But her demeanor had changed. For lack of a better word, he thought she was getting too big for her britches. Then she started wearing clothes more fitting of a woman than a girl. He didn't like anything tight on her, anything that accentuated curves or made men take notice. He may have grown up and spent his whole life as a conservative Lutheran, but he'd been a teenager, too, full of the lusts and desires that he just knew teenage boys were directing at his little girl.

He didn't say anything, at least when Patricia was around. But one morning after Patricia had left for the Test Site, Wendy's nylons set him off.

Women wear nylons. They do it for one reason: to get men to look at their legs. Is that what she wanted? To have men ogling and desiring her? His thirteen-year-old girl having sex?

"You little whore!" he said. "Get those fucking nylons off. Now!"

He slid his belt off his waist and doubled it over, making a snapping sound as he pulled the ends and made the leather strips smack together.

"Get them off!"

"I will! I will!" she replied.

She sat on the kitchen floor, tearing them as she ripped them off.

"You want to be a whore? Is that what you want? Is that how we taught you?"

She stood up and gave him the ball of nylon, then ran to her bedroom and slammed the door. She cried, but only for a minute. She took a deep breath. She suddenly felt an emptiness that comes from the realization that your dad thinks you're worthless. Michael came to mind and how isolated and alone he must have felt for so many years.

Wendy stepped out of her room, walked down the hallway to the bathroom, and closed the door. She turned on the faucet. Her dad's razor was in the medicine cabinet. She screwed it open and pulled out the blade. With toilet paper, she wrapped one side so she could grip it tight without slicing her fingers.

Then she sliced her wrists. A little force didn't work, so she pressed hard and slid the blade at the same time, letting it cut deep enough to break the wall of the artery pumping blood to her hand. It shocked her, how high the blood shot when the artery broke. Then she did her right wrist.

Turned off the water. Opened the door.

Her dad wasn't in his bedroom when she walked in. She sat down and called Emily. "I cut my wrists," she said.

Then John Watson saw her, blood pooling at her feet. "My God, what did you do? What did you do?" His ashen face was flecked with his daughter's arterial blood drops.

Michael jumped into action, grabbed some belts and tightened them around Wendy's arms. Someone called Patricia. She raced from the Test Site, arriving at the hospital just after John and his fading daughter.

Rushed into an emergency room, Wendy lost control.

"Motherfuckers! Bastards! You fuckers!" she screamed at the four nurses who held her down as a doctor patched her wrists.

Stitched up, sedated, and secured to her bed, she watched in a daze at mom crying and dad sitting with head in hands.

A Las Vegas detective broke the reverie.

"All you fuckers, fuck off," she slurred.

"You don't deserve these parents," the cop spat.

"Fuck you."

Wendy spent the next two weeks under psychiatric evaluation in Child Haven, a county-run facility typically reserved for the children of parents under arrest or otherwise deemed unfit. Anger and hatred tinged her every thought, every word. Even she didn't understand it. The Watsons weren't a religious family, but she thought a demon had possessed her. Why couldn't she let it go? Where was her laughter?

"So, how we doing today?" came the counselor's morning refrain.

"Go get fucked."

After two weeks, the counselor gave up. Wendy didn't want help, he concluded. Nothing he could do. Wendy wished the suicide had taken. Nothing had changed except she now had stitches, would bear the scars for life and she still felt empty and angry.

At school, kids made sure she saw the disgust on their faces. They asked how she could ever do something like that to her parents. They laughed at her. It helped in a way. It helped her build an impermeable wall.

Walking the halls, she could look at anyone walking by without ever looking into their eyes. She looked through them, beyond them, never at them. After weeks, she owned that mask. In the mirror, she barely recognized who looked back.

Solid friends fell away, choosing others with a greater chance of amassing a higher popularity quotient. Parents forbade their kids to hang around Wendy; afraid that whatever she had might rub off.

But older kids had no problem with Wendy. Like her, they knew it was all bullshit—school, cliques, classes, and popularity contests.

Jane, a friend, became their ringleader. Wendy cruised many miles in the low-riders polished and retooled by

Jane's friends, many out of high school and working in the casinos.

It was 1970. Drugs took root in Las Vegas and never left. Mescaline brought Jane, Wendy, and their mutual friend, Katie, to stomach-aching laughter at a Three Dog Night concert. Once they shot a syringe full of nothing into their arms, then laughed at the air bubble that formed under Katie's skin.

Wendy's parents didn't mind that the girls were older. Wendy was raised Lutheran while Jane and Katie were Mormon. But John and Patricia Watson cared little about the different theologies. They only saw that their little girl was going to Mormon services three times a week. Jesus or Moroni, who cared as long as she followed the name into church and off the streets?

At least that's what Wendy let them believe. They might step foot in the door of the church, just to say they went. Then they'd flee to the desert to smoke pot. Same thing on school days. Wendy needed the bond with her friends, even as she felt her already shaky foundation start to crumble. This, too, was at a time when the Vietnam War, which her mom was intimately aware of as a high-level military employee, raged on. Much of Las Vegas depended upon, and suffered from, the ravages of the war.

At the same time, racial tensions in Las Vegas exploded. For decades, black residents of Las Vegas endured codified discrimination. Until the late '60s, banks would rarely consider home loans for black residents who wanted to buy outside of a ten-block-square area near downtown called the "Westside." Neither could they own businesses outside the area. Schools were unabashedly segregated along white and black lines. Racial tensions boiled over,

first in high schools where fights began to break out between the few blacks allowed to attend white schools.
Then, in October 1969, a two-day riot erupted just a mile
or so east of Charleston Heights, Wendy's neighborhood.
Marauding gangs burned buildings and destroyed whatever
was at hand. Months later, local political leaders drafted a
graduated desegregation plan. In the early '70s, housing
and business ownership restrictions eased, and blacks
were allowed to live and own businesses throughout Las
Vegas, not just in a confined area.

Racial anger ebbed, but on the nightly news Wendy
watched with fascination the lush green jungles of Vietnam
colored red with blood as news cameras captured young
men pulling bodies onto gurneys and hauling them into
helicopters. Her parents didn't talk about it, but Vietnam
seeped into so many sectors of Las Vegas with so many
residents working at Nellis or the Test Site or Groom Lake.
War meant longer hours and more stress at work, where
indecision or the wrong decision could cost the lives of
Americans thousands of miles away. Only 500,000 people
lived in the state in 1970, but between 1965 and the end
of 1969, 126 Nevadans died in Vietnam, 67 of those from
the Las Vegas area.

So kids were doing drugs, drugs that parents hadn't
tried and fewer understood. All of it amounted to a worry
on par with playing hooky from school. The order of the
day was getting up, going to work, coming home, and
waking up to do it again, and hoping your kids knew right
from wrong, because talking about drugs wasn't in the
handbook for most families.

On Wendy's fifteenth birthday, friends gave her "reds" as
a gift. Downers. She took them all. Then a boy took her

to his house. She passed out, and when she awoke, she pushed off her boyfriend, who had fallen asleep on top of her. She stood and it hurt between her legs. Flecks of dried blood clung to her leg and his bed sheet. He had raped her.

She said nothing. When she got home late, Patricia Watson sensed something wrong. She asked but Wendy said "nothing." Then she lay on her bed and cried, ashamed and guilty. Maybe she really was a whore, like her dad said? Who else but a whore would someone feel okay about raping? She took all those pills, after all. She practically invited it. She wasn't blind—she saw the way grown men twice her age looked at her, smiled and winked at her. Before, she only saw them as being gentlemanly to a little girl, the same as the drunks around Rocking Horse Ranch when they cheered her on during a race. Then one day she noticed the smiles had become leers as they scanned her body, from head to toe. Is that the kind of attention she wanted? What kind of girl wants that?

Maybe the cop was right: She didn't deserve her parents. They wouldn't understand anyway. Dad would simply shake his head. Mom would cry. She felt more alone than ever.

Then she met Teddy Binion.

CHAPTER FOUR

Americans don't easily find beauty in the rocky, brown soil and thorned plant world of the Mojave Desert. This isn't the kind of place where people naturally sink roots and start a life. If anything, it's the kind of place envisioned at the end of life, a place where everything but the most resilient die. In the early '70s, nuclear bombs were still being detonated sixty-five miles north of the city. A few decades later, congressional leaders saw the desert north of Las Vegas as a wasteland suitable for a nuclear waste dump. Transplants from the Midwest and other parts of the country watered their lawns to the point of overflow to re-create the verdant landscapes of their childhood homes. They saw the desert no differently than anyone else, using it as their dump for old cars and washing machines that became targets for weekend warriors. "Shallow desert grave" became a cliché but it began because stories of hikers finding bodies in the desert always seemed to be turning up in the newspapers. It isn't hard to understand why the Mojave Desert, at a glance lifeless and seemingly incapable of sustaining life, embodied hell for many.

For Wendy, the desert was none of that. It was sanctuary. The scent of sage shot her back to Red running as hard as he could and the freedom they had together, made her look to the ever-blue sky and lizards on tippy-toes skittering from shade to shade over burning sand.

But Wendy wasn't ten anymore. She was fifteen, she

didn't have Red, and school became an afterthought to
her and her friends.

And then there was Fremont Street.

She could stand for hours in front of Woolworth's at
Fremont and Main, the place downtown tourists ended up
for Alka-Seltzer or a newspaper or simply to take in the
familiar aroma of Woolworth popcorn, reminding them
that they still had a home to return to no matter what they
had just done over the weekend in Las Vegas.

For Wendy and her friends, Woolworth's became the
new hangout after it got a photo booth. They'd wander
into the store to look at costume jewelry, then put a quarter into the booth, cram inside, and make funny faces in
front of the camera. They'd get a good laugh at the silly
photos that dropped out a minute later. Woolworth's also
provided safe perch for gazing east into Fremont Street,
where miles of neon painted the drunks and high-heeled
women as they stumbled into the road and reflected off
the high-gloss finish of trolling vehicles. People-watching
here became sport as the girls tried to one-up each other
by pointing out the oddest sight of the night.

The novelty of watching quickly waned. Now they wanted into the casinos so they could see for themselves the
transformation of tourist into debaucher. They talked daily
about how they'd walk in, feigning bored disdain, maybe
pause to watch someone at the blackjack table, advise a
tourist to hit on 15, then let some young fella light their
cigarettes.

Of all the Fremont casinos, the Horseshoe was tops on
the list. Its founder, Benny Binion, was a former horse
trader and bootlegger from Dallas—where he also had

been convicted of one killing and acquitted of another after a judge ruled he had killed in self-defense.

The Binion name in Dallas carried the kind of respect that's born of fear and power. Benny ran an illegal lottery in the late 1920s into the 30s. He was also a bootlegger, selling alcohol illegally during Prohibition. Tom met Benny in Dallas and started working for him, he told Wendy, after he ran away from home in his mid-teens. Tom also met his future wife, Mary Lou, in Texas. Around 1936, when Tom was nineteen, Binion sent him to his ranch in Colorado to grow hops and highly profitable marijuana. But in 1939, just after Mary Lou gave birth to Gramby, Benny sent for Tom again. A gang war had begun, and Benny needed Tom back in Dallas to fight off rivals, including the Chicago Outfit, which was trying to take over his empire. Tom went to Dallas and left his mom, Stella, in Colorado to oversee the ranch.

Binion, though, was losing the battle and was looking for other places to set up. So he sent Tom to Las Vegas in the early '40s. There, Tom learned the sheet metal trade and got involved in the union.

With fight-first, negotiate-later tactics learned from Binion, Tom's notoriety in Las Vegas grew quickly. But he had established a foothold in the desert city. In the late '40s, Benny, his wife and children, a brood that would grow to five, moved to Las Vegas and lived with Tom until they got a home of their own on Bonanza Road. Their bond became one that lasted the rest of Tom's life, even after Tom married Wendy some twenty years later.

Binion's Horseshoe Club opened in 1951 and it was a sensation, its name becoming synonymous countrywide with cheap drinks, food, high-stakes gambling, and a wink-and-nod acceptance of just about every illicit activity you never found in middle America. Benny served time in prison in the mid-'50s for tax evasion stemming from his activities in Texas. To pay his legal fees, he sold his casino interests. The Binion family in the '60s purchased majority rights back, but Benny never got another gaming license after prison. Other family members ran the Horseshoe; Benny became a paid consultant.

To the girls, Benny's son, Teddy, was a local celebrity. His toothy Hollywood smile emanated a country boy sincerity. At twenty-seven in 1970, he exuded an aw-shucks cowboy appeal—his thinness hiding ferocity in the way of farmers whose scrawny arms mask a steeliness capable of breaking a jaw with a single punch.

Not that Teddy was a fighter. He didn't have to be—bodyguards or family friends could be called on to fight for him. Besides, he loved casinos and the legal license it afforded to get away with almost anything without raising a fist. Casino appeal went both ways. Customers loved the spit-on-the-floor style of the Horseshoe and felt it offered a sanctum from the laws and mores of society. Hookers? Drugs? Blind drunkenness? Fine, just don't cause a ruckus.

If the girls could get into a casino, the Horseshoe was the one.

"Just walk in like we own the place," Wendy said and started walking down the street. She stiffened her back and straightened her neck to be taller, donned her mask of haughty indifference. What did she care—they walk in and what's the worst that can happen? They get thrown out and go back to Woolworth's.

Their fail-safe excuse: The Horseshoe had just installed an ice cream parlor. Sure, they were under aged, they'd say if stopped, but did they have to wait for their parents to get a simple ice cream cone?

"What are you doing?" Kate asked, running across the street after Wendy, who was striding toward the casino. "What are we—are we doing it?"

"Come on," Wendy told her. "We'll go into the gift shop first, then walk into the casino."

Wendy strutted in while Kate kept her head down, eyes darting back and forth while she pulled hair over her ears to hide her face.

As they entered the casino and a wall of bitter cigar smoke stung their eyes, they stifled the urge to cough. They broke through and began to smile as their eyes adjusted to the dim light. The casino's innards came into focus. Gleaming metal frames encased rows of slot machines, all of them functionally designed: coin pan at the bottom, three reels in the middle, and payouts on top. Drop a quarter, pull the noisy arm on the side, and lose. Or win enough so the dropping coins hit the pan with enough clang to entice others to try.

Row after row of machines with row after row of robotic players smoking cigarettes, pulling the arms, and staring at the reels. Real money was on the line. This suited Wendy fine; she didn't want anyone to notice. But someone did.

"Hey, hey, hold on, girls," someone called behind them. The voice was loud but playful.

Both froze. And turned to face Teddy Binion.

"Can I see some IDs?" he said, his eyes narrowed in mock seriousness. "We can't have kids in here, even kids as sexy as you two."

"Well, I, let me find it here," Wendy dug into her purse. Kate did the same. "We just wanted some ice cream."

Binion burst into laughter.

"Come on, I'm just kidding! You girls are fine. Welcome to the Horseshoe. You girls want to go over to the new ice cream parlor, have an ice cream cone with me?"

"Sure, why not?" Wendy said.

After sitting in the parlor licking on ice cream cones, Teddy asked the girls, "Would you like to have a tour of the Horseshoe Club"?

"Yes, that would be fun, Mr. Binion," Wendy replied.

"Call me Teddy. You girls don't have to be formal with me, I just help my dad run this place. Hey, you girls look old enough to drink, would you like a drink?" Binion said.

"Why not," Wendy answered, "but are you sure it's okay for us to drink?"

"Of course. Come on, have some fun!"

He ordered tequila sunrises that came with umbrellas. They sipped as he walked and talked. Wendy had never met anyone so warm, so full of fun. He maneuvered himself so he was walking next to her. From a lifetime around gamblers, the youngest son of Benny had a card player's knack for reading his prey. He didn't bother with Kate, who was still a child and very much under Wendy's control. In Wendy, he saw a stunning beauty who wouldn't believe it; afraid of the world but unwilling to admit it. And someone who wanted to belong and would never forsake the one who loved her. She was loyal and a fighter.

He touched Wendy's arm, then held it longer than a touch, checking to see if she kept smiling. Then he slipped an arm around her waist. Wendy didn't blush. She thought someone older would lean into him, so that's what she did, walking like she expected that arm. Kate walked apart, arms crossed, unblinking, scared and ignored.

The next day, Wendy skipped school and played with Teddy. He gave her coins to throw into slot machines. Let her throw dice at the craps table. Bought her dinner at the café. Introduced her to staff and gamblers as "my gal, Wendy." He electrified her. He never took his focus off of her, no matter who walked by in any kind of mini skirt. She felt like his gal, like the most important person in the place.

When she tired and had to go home early in the evening, he pooh-poohed the very idea of leaving. He gave her the key to her own room in the hotel above the casino to nap until she wanted to come back down. Alone. He was the perfect gentleman. Close to midnight, he paid for a cab to drive her home.

She fell in love. Teddy never asked for anything but gave so much. New clothes. Bracelets and a necklace made of gold. After a few weeks, she asked Teddy if he wanted to nap with her one late afternoon. That first time, all they did was sleep. Wendy wanted to make him happy. He didn't push it. She was fifteen. He seemed boyish, almost shy. She made love to him because she wanted to. She mostly stopped going to school, stopped talking to her friend. She only wanted him.

Teddy only came out at night, sleeping most of the day. If Wendy went to school, she'd skip afternoon classes, go home when no one was there, get dolled up, and get to the casino as Teddy made his casino entrance, always smiling, always full of energy. They'd do lines of coke in a tiny, hideaway office on the casino floor, then wade into the casino night.

She made friends with all the regulars who cherished her laughter and shoulder rubs and goofy jokes, rekindling an innocence they had lost long ago to losses, wins, and the winner-take-all gravity of gambling.

Teddy liked having her around, too. Loved her energy. When they snorted cocaine, he always made sure never to let her overdo it, which she took as love. He wanted her to be able to function, to visit the men at the tables, to let them feed off her unlined youth and energy. She could be so much more. He had plans for her.

Wendy's parents had plans, too.

As busy as Patricia Watson was at work, and John Watson was trying to hold his trucking business together while nursing a serious drinking habit, they weren't entirely out of the loop. Friends started talking. Did they know Wendy was seen at the Horseshoe the other night? And Teddy was all over her? And wasn't she supposed to be in school, anyhow? How was she getting her homework done? She never called Katie anymore.

Skipping afternoon classes one day to get ready for Teddy, Wendy was surprised to find her mom and dad at the house.

"Let's get in the car and go for a ride," her dad said.

Michael and Wendy got into the car. Michael had just been released from juvenile hall. It would be another year before he turned seventeen, when he became one of the youngest people in Nevada at the time to be sentenced to prison.

"You're staying away from the Horseshoe and staying at Child Haven tonight," her dad said. "If we can't keep you away from that casino, they will."

The county-run facility for abused and neglected kids was ten minutes away. But they never got there. As the car came to a stop at a light, Wendy yanked on the door release, jumped out of the car, and ran.

"Go get her!" her dad screamed at Michael.

Michael dashed after her, chasing her behind a house. She was stuck. She couldn't get over a fence. Michael walked toward her quickly.

"Get away from me! Let me go!"

Michael put a finger to his lips to shush her. Then he clasped his hands to make a foothold and helped her over the fence.

"Bye, Wendy."

"Goodbye, Michael."

She ran to a friend's house with life-and-death urgency. Plain and simple, her parents were embarrassed because she was keeping company with someone who really cared for her, magnifying their own failure as parents in the process.

"Take a cab and get over here right away," Teddy told her on the phone.

Wendy's heart jumped. Teddy knew because he felt the same. He needed her as much as she needed him.

She slept in a Horseshoe room and he climbed in with her well after midnight. Her mom and dad reported her as a runaway, telling police they believed she was with Teddy or at the Horseshoe. Police probably already knew, close as the sheriff was to Benny Binion. They reported back to the Watsons: She hasn't turned up anywhere yet.

For a week, Teddy bounced Wendy between the casino, his house, and the homes of friends. Then he rented her a studio apartment a few blocks from the casino. The refrigerator was filled with food before she arrived and the closet was jammed with clothes, some of the sort she had never worn before: evening gowns with long slits up the leg, knee-high white boots with three-inch heels, sequined bell bottoms, a fluorescent rainbow of hot pants. Several boxes of jewelry made of gold, silver, and gems.

Wendy had the power of the Binion's, an old, respected, and feared casino family, to keep her family and the police away. The Horseshoe didn't merely instill the fear of violence without punishment into police officers; it bankrolled some of the police department's operations. Benny Binion was more than happy to supply police with the bundles of cash needed for whatever undercover drug scheme they were working on.

Energized by an endless supply of cocaine, Wendy flitted and flirted around the casino with men who welcomed her with smiles, hugs, and the occasional ass-grab. It didn't bother her—they knew she was "Teddy's girl." She felt part of a team but with an influence that far exceeded the casino waitresses, dealers, and pit bosses. She did, after all, sleep with the boss.

"Wendy Binion," she wrote over and over on Horseshoe napkins.

Teddy, though, made it very clear about his intentions. He not only wined and dined other women, but his daily interaction with Wendy dwindled. Soon, he talked to her through security guards, who would tell her "Teddy wants" her to massage the shoulders of a particular poker player or sit next to an influential blackjack player. Make them feel at home. Her thinking toward their relationship evolved, too. Teddy was a busy man. He couldn't reach her every time he wanted to say something. She still knew that deep down he cared.

By the middle of what would have been Wendy's

sophomore year, police turned up the heat. Wendy's mom called the department relentlessly. Las Vegas was small and many worked at the Test Site, where people told Patricia rumors of Wendy being at the casino with Teddy Binion, dressing like a tramp. She started making a pest of herself at Binion's, visiting nightly and roaming around the tables asking about her daughter. She never found Wendy due to the casino's efficient silent alarm—bellmen alerted floormen who alerted Wendy, who would sneak up the casino's back stairs to hide in a room always left open for her.

But having a mom nosing around all the time wasn't good for business.

"We have to get you out of here," Teddy finally told Wendy. "I won't let them take you."

He sent her to Texas with Charlie Briscoe. The Briscoes were longtime family friends. Charlie piloted a long, black Lincoln Continental that he kept a cool sixty-eight degrees. Nevertheless, the underarms of his shirts, all of them with steel-tipped collars, soaked through. Tall with impenetrable black hair, cheekbones like rocks in his burnt skin, Charlie turned women's heads. Wendy thought him good looking until she spent a few days sitting two feet away from him. He ate nothing when they stopped but drank bottle after bottle of Coca-Cola while popping pills. A life of frustration or anger creased his brow in an upside-down T, even when he laughed, which was precisely once when he shook his head at the cloudburst that opened on his freshly washed car. He chewed his lower lip, gnawed his fingernails to nubs, and rolled tiny balls of paper with his thumb and index finger, letting them drop to the floor or litter the car seat. His brake knee bounced without stop. He only talked to say they were getting gas. And he never slept.

She'd be gone for a month, maybe two, Teddy promised before she got into Charlie's car. "And here's the best part—all you have to do is drink lemonade in the shade and ride horses all day.

On the road from Nevada to Texas, the Southwest slowly morphed from Nevada's dried-shit brown hue to the light jade-greens and violets of New Mexico to the straw-gold grasses of Texas, dotted with trees stuck forever in the middle of vast flatlands.

All of it was new and exciting to a girl who had never left Nevada.

Almost two days later, Charlie pulled into a massive ranch outside Dallas. More than a dozen horses ran over an expanse of fenced yellow grass stretching as far as she could see. Teddy had told the truth. He did love her, she thought.

For two weeks, she did just as Teddy said: drank lemonade, cooled herself in the wet Gulf Coast breezes and shade, and ran the horses.

One night, she came in through the unlocked front door to find Charlie at the kitchen table with a pile of receipts.

"You're going to be here a little while longer, so you'll have to work a little to earn your keep," he said. "Just until you get back to Las Vegas."

She was fine with that. She was at her best meeting new people. "I'll do whatever you want me to do," she said.

Charlie moved his head until he caught her eyes. "Yes, you will."

She blushed as he surveyed her body, stopping at her hips. He wondered what fifteen looked like under those jeans—more importantly, what other men would think of someone so scrawny and how she'd hold up.

"We'll start you tomorrow."

CHAPTER FIVE

The next day Charlie smiled at the breakfast table. He swigged from a light-green Coke bottle and popped a pill. Wendy had some potato chips and a Coke. Charlie's aura never changed. It was always black.

"Ride the horses all day if you want. You'll start around dinner time."

Which, to Wendy, meant waitressing. She was excited. She'd never had a real job but she knew she was good at meeting people and making them smile. Plus, the idea of making her own money and having a job was bound to convince her parents she was beyond high school.

Light makeup, an airy, flowered dress, and bobbing curls in her long brown hair, she was ready and giddy as Charlie opened the door to the Continental. Another girl staying in the house, Patty, got in, too.

Ten miles later, they pulled into the gravel parking lot of a flat-roofed motel, rectangular with a courtyard in the middle that all the doors faced. She couldn't make out the name because the sign had long ago been shattered with rocks or gunshot or both. Where's the restaurant? she wondered.

Charlie threw the car into park and released a deep breath that trembled. Wendy blushed when he turned and stared at her legs, then lifted her chin with a finger to look her in the eye.

"You know, Teddy told me you are like a young filly

thoroughbred that needs to be broken in. I think he was right."

He got out, walked around the Lincoln, and opened Wendy's door. He yanked her out by the arm and walked fast to the motel office, dragging her along.

"We need a key," he told the large man behind the desk.

With Patty trailing behind, he dragged Wendy to one of the rooms. He closed and bolted the door.

"Get your clothes off."

"What?"

"I said, get your clothes off, goddammit."

"Wendy, just do it," Patty said.

Wendy stripped to her panties and bra while Charlie took all of his clothes off, facing her naked. He looked at her and snorted at the fact that she still had on her underwear. Made no difference. He walked up to her, grabbed her by the shoulders, and shoved her onto the bed.

"Please, this is a mistake," Wendy said. Tears stung her eyes. "Call Teddy. I'm only fifteen."

Charlie chuckled. He grabbed her by the hair, pulled aside her panties, and forced himself inside. Patty told her where to put her hands. Then Charlie got up, and Patty told her how to give a blow job to make him cum faster, to get it over with so she could get to the next customer.

"This is no mistake," Charlie said. "This is your job."

❖ ❖ ❖

When he finished, Charlie took her by the back of the neck and walked to Room 1 adjacent to the office. Unlocking the door, he shoved her in and locked it from the outside. The room had two beds. Two girls sat on the beds smoking and watching television. One had a black eye. They each wore days-old lingerie—all in garters, one with a pink see-through nightie with white fluff on the hem that hung about ass-high; another covered her naked body with a red silken robe that didn't shine anymore.

They all looked older, must be in their thirties, Wendy thought. They came to Wendy's aid, settled her down, put Band-Aids on her cuts.

"They won't let you cry," Patty said. "If they see you cry, they'll hit you 'til you stop."

Bob Barker on *Truth or Consequences* was about to surprise a young wife by reuniting her with her husband smuggled in from Vietnam for just this dramatic moment. A bouncing wife and husky Jarhead filled the screen that entranced the other two girls.

Patty stayed in the room with them. She had to work, too. She told Wendy how it went: When the pimp in the front office called the room where the girls were held, the girl whose turn it was would pick up the phone, and the pimp would tell her which room to go to and what the customer had paid for. The pimp also explained how much time he expected the girl to be in the room with the customer. The pimp then would buzz open the room the girls were in, and the girl whose turn it was would walk to the customer's room and knock on the door. If the guy didn't like her, he would call the front office and ask for a replacement.

Patty went through the terminology: blow job, a lay job, a hand job, and the colorfully named "twirl around the world," a pricier service not unlike a meal deal at a fast-food restaurant—burger, fries, drink, and maybe some kind of quickie dessert.

They each might see six or more men a night, more on Fridays and Saturdays. They could tell which Fridays were paydays, because they'd be exhausted by the end of the night.

There was no escape. All the rooms formed a box with their doors facing the interior. You got into the interior through the office. And you got out through the same office door. That door only opened when Tex buzzed it open. They were trapped. If Wendy tried to tell any of the "tricks" what was going on, or if she tried to escape, she would "be taken out back and shot."

"Well, this is where we're at," Patty said. "You don't have any money, and you're not going to get out of here unless you work. So work hard. If you don't, there's a lot of girls who have disappeared and are buried in a hole out back."

The girls never saw money. They subsisted on junk food, coffee, and soda. Tex unlocked the door in the mornings and put down a tray of coffee cups, sandwiches, and soda. Twinkies were hoarded and saved for their alone time after they had showered and were lying on the bed dreaming of the day they would get out.

Two of the girls were runaways in their late teens. Patty, a tall, natural redhead with farm-fresh white skin, was there by choice. Despite her perpetual black eyes and arms red and swollen beneath fishnet sleeves, Patty called the man with the fists her boyfriend. He was Charlie.

She later confided to Wendy that her dad, a judge in another county, had threatened to kill Charlie and ran him out of the county.

Patty followed Charlie.

"I love him," she later told Wendy, confiding that she believed her judge-father was only trying to deny her happiness by forcing Charlie out of the county.

Three hours after Wendy's lesson, watching the girls

come and go from the room, the phone rang again, and Patty told Wendy it was her turn. Still shaking and hurting from what Charlie had done to her earlier, Wendy wiped her tears and picked up the phone. Tex, the pimp in the front office, told Wendy what the customer paid for and what room to walk to. When Tex buzzed the door to let Wendy out, she pushed open the door, thinking to herself; "I'm getting out of here!" As she walked into the courtyard, she noticed it was almost sunset. She thought that maybe she could run. But after scoping out the property, she realized there was no place to go.

This can't be happening, she thought. How did this happen?

Wendy walked to the room that Tex had directed her to and knocked on the door. When the door opened there stood a middle-aged man with a cowboy hat. He was in his underwear and wearing cowboy boots. He looked at her and, with a heavy Texas drawl, said, "Come on in, you little cutie." Wendy stepped into the room and stood still as the man took off his hat and threw it on the bed.

"My name is Woody," he said. "Turn around so I can see what I paid for."

Still in shock, Wendy turned slowly around, as the man's eyes surveyed every inch of her body.

"Boy, you are a pretty little thing, aren't you?"

Wendy started to cry, and the man's demeanor changed. "What the heck is this?" he said. "What's wrong with you, little lady?"

She then remembered to be quiet and do what she was told to do. She responded, "Oh nothing. I've just had a rough day, that's all."

"Well, let's wipe them tears and have us a little party!"

Woody reeked of tar and salty sweat. She took him to the bathroom and tried to clean him up before he got what he paid for.

When it was over, Wendy walked back to the room where the girls were and knocked on the door. When it buzzed open, she walked into the room and collapsed on the bed. She curled herself into a ball and cried hysterically.

"Hush now," Patty whispered. "Tex is going to be calling the room any minute to see how you acted. Stop crying and pull yourself together."

❖ ❖ ❖

Every night Wendy paced the room, then lay on her bed crying until she fell asleep. She tried to wash and brush the taste of all those men from her mouth and body

Three weeks passed. Wendy's already wispy body had lost ten pounds. Patty felt sorry for her. She wasn't making it. She'd seen what happened to other girls who couldn't handle the rigors of the job. Many of them simply disappeared.

"This life isn't for you. I can't get you out of here, but you'll never get out of here if you don't make extra money," Patty whispered to her one night. "You've got to do more. Do extra for tips. Hide the money, and when you have enough for a bus ticket, I'll get you out of here."

For two weeks, Wendy choked back the wretch as she kindly asked if, perhaps, the customer would want to do something a little extra to her or get something more from her? It'd only cost an extra $10, maybe $20. In two weeks, she saved about $80; just enough to cover the three-day bus ride to Las Vegas.

One window faced the inner courtyard. The only opening to the outside was a tiny window in the bathroom.

Shut. But that tiny window in the shower might work. Late at night, Wendy and Patty broke the window, Wendy squeezed in, and Patty pushed hard to get her out. Wendy ran until the motel lights faded behind her and she felt blacktop under her feet. A cowboy in a pickup drove her to a nearby Greyhound station, which amounted to a matchbox-sized office and two or three people waiting for a ride. Wendy had just enough for the ticket, with almost a dollar left over for a big bag of Cheetos.

In electric orange hot pants, three-inch platform shoes, and a windbreaker over a T-shirt, she sat in the cold plastic chair and waited.

Teddy let this happen, she stewed. He said she was "his girl." She felt part of the Binion family. She couldn't wrap her mind around the idea that he could do this to her after all they'd shared, after he'd helped her escape her parents, bought her all those nice things.

Wendy didn't want to cry, felt she didn't deserve tears, had no reason to feel pity for herself. She had become the whore her dad accused her of being. Only a whore could have done the things she had done in that motel. Sure, she hated every minute. But she still did it. Why hadn't she broken through a window earlier?

And now what? She could never face her parents. She had abandoned her friends. For all she knew, Teddy was back at the Horseshoe joking with the gamblers she thought were friends, telling them where she was and what she was doing and how she'd be "real ready" when she got back.

At least, though, shame went out the window at the Horseshoe. They knew her there. Besides, she had no-where else to turn.

Her bus had just pulled up and was getting gassed, when Charlie's black Continental pulled in. He jumped out of the car. Patty stayed in the front passenger seat, sporting a new black eye.

"Get your ass in the fucking car or I'll kill you," he hissed at Wendy, clenching his teeth.

"If you lay one hand on me, I'll scream my head off."

Charlie seethed. He looked around. Some Mexican women with brown paper bags full of clothes and tamales for their trip looked at them. The ticket clerk stared at him through a Plexiglas partition.

"I said get in the fucking car!"

No way was Wendy going to get in the car with him. Charlie was a former boxer who had lost his boxing license after killing someone in the ring. Wendy knew he would have either beaten her to death or within a hair of it.

Just then a tall man in a cowboy hat started walking toward Charlie.

"Goddammit," Charlie hissed. He turned and got back in the car. Gravel flew from the rear wheels as he sped away.

"You okay, ma'am?" the cowboy asked.

"I am, thank you."

Over the three-day bus ride, Wendy nibbled every half-hour at a few Cheetos, until the lights of Las Vegas came into view and she had the freedom to eat a whole handful.

The warmth of the Horseshoe's café awaited.

So did Teddy Binion.

CHAPTER SIX

"**C**harlie's a dead man."

In the café, just feet from the table games, Teddy sat in the booth where his dad sat and held court daily with lawyers, politicians, union leaders, and regular Joes who came to him with offers, pleas, supplications, thanks, or just to say hi and honor his presence.

The young casino operator did his best to calm Wendy, who couldn't stop crying, her quavering voice signaling a potential breakdown. A security guard said nothing but stood by looking worried. A black bellman shook his head in disgust.

"This isn't right," the bellman said. "Your old man would have a fit if he knew this had happened."

None of the waitresses said a word. They weren't allowed to. Teddy always pulled Wendy away from the other female employees if she saw them talking. He wanted her completely separate from them and their Las Vegas lives of husbands and kids, and totally absorbed into his world and the Horseshoe.

Hardened as they were—and completely open to the notion of prostitution in the casino—the bellman, security, and other male employees stuck together, as long as sticking together wouldn't jeopardize their jobs.

Many young, beautiful girls had passed through Teddy's life before Wendy. They'd swoon in the glamour and attention and gifts that Teddy lavished on them. Then, somehow, they'd see his attentions as license to treat the employees like garbage. But Wendy wasn't like those other part-time Teddy girlfriends. Not only did she practically live in the casino, she was there so often that she never acted as if she were better than they were. She never saw herself as anything more than Teddy's "stringy-haired little girl." The very idea of turning up a nose at others, seeing herself as prettier, as is or better than anyone, never entered her mind.

"I'm sending someone down there to kill that son of a bitch," Teddy told them. He wanted everyone to hear, even though Wendy already knew he wouldn't do it, that he was a liar, that she was set up to convert her, to "break her in."

Wendy did, however, know one thing: She had leverage, born of the fact that the casino workers liked her. This kind of concern wasn't typical. She knew it, and Teddy knew it.

"Teddy, I want a job, a real job," she pleaded.

Without a thought, as if he already had it planned, Teddy waved Natty over to their table. Natty was the casino's loan shark and poker player. Salt-and-pepper hair, plaid sport coat, white leather belt, white penny loafers. The top three buttons of his dress shirt undone, a gold Star of David hung from his neck and nestled in his visible chest hair that grew like fur spawned from his diet of smokes and black coffee. Like most of the men at the casino, he wore a pinky ring.

Always respectful and a soft talker, Wendy liked Natty. He was there every day. A family man from Chicago, loan sharking earned him enough to support him and his wife.

"Hey, boss, what can I do ya for?"

Wendy needs a new wardrobe, Teddy said. Natty whisked himself away and returned with $2,000 in hundred-dollar bills. He wrote it down in a little black book.

The prospect of real work excited Wendy. She'd never return to school, of that she was certain. She didn't want to go back to the ridicule and sneers that she faced after cutting her wrists. Whatever Teddy had in mind, she was certain it would be honest work, a way to make a steady income. Plus, since she had no rent and ate for free at the casino, she could save to pay off Natty. She'd erase Texas and make her mom proud.

"You'll need a new wardrobe and a place to stay," Teddy said. "Go with her to get some clothes."

The bellman took the money. He knew what to buy. All the bellman did, because they worked together on the side as pimps, all with the approval of their bosses at several different casinos. One bellman might call the bellman from another casino to give him a tip, for a fee, about a prospective john coming to the casino.

Wendy bought fishnet tops with bell-bottomed sleeves that tied at the waist to show her navel. Low-cut pants. More fishnet leggings. One of the crop-tops that tied at the waist was handmade, very expensive, and with the electric blue bell bottoms the bellman picked out to go with it, it made Teddy and all the other casino men comment about how sexy it made her look.

Then she had a short course in how to treat a customer. Most of the gamblers were married, so there'd be no open shows of affection. She could smile, sit very close, even rub their legs under the table after a winning hand. But nothing else. Not yet.

She wasn't allowed to drink alcohol. Teddy hated sloppy, drunken women. She had to sit up straight, fold hands in her lap, never put them on the table.

"Just sit there as pretty as you can with style and grace,"
he said. "You're a Binion Girl now. You have to act like one."

❖ ❖ ❖

The Horseshoe held its third World Series of Poker in May
1972 with a top prize of $20,000. Eight men started and
cowboy Amarillo Slim won. Through most of the match,
Wendy sat next to Slim or rubbed his shoulders. His "good
luck charm," he called her. As flashbulbs popped, she
posed on his lap for photos.

"Let's go to a movie," he said.

They saw *The Godfather*, which had opened two months
earlier, at Cinema 1-2-3 on Fremont Street, a couple blocks
east of the Horseshoe. But for the neon, the sky had grown
dark by the time Michael had closed the door on his
wife and completed his transformation into the Don. Cars
streamed up and down Fremont. Slim put on his cowboy
hat, reached into his pocket, pulled out a thousand dollars,
and gave it to Wendy.

"You're a good kid," he said. "Get away from this. Go
home."

He called her a cab. Wendy told the cabbie to drive a
few blocks, then return to the Horseshoe. She couldn't
face her mom. Not yet. Maybe never.

❖ ❖ ❖

The next day, one of the local papers described the girl
sitting on Amarillo Slim's lap as a "stunning brunette" and
Slim's "good luck charm." Natty ran up to Wendy with the
paper.

"Look at our gal," he said. "She hit the paper!"

Wendy blushed and smiled as a crowd gathered around.
For the first time, she felt appreciated, even loved.

The next day, Natty was Natty, reminding Wendy about

the money she owed. "Got any of that money yet, Wendy, got any of that money?" he'd ask.

He hung around like cigarette smoke or the stale meat smell stuck on the carpeting and walls from the mountains of prime rib dinners, which cost only $1.18 on Wednesdays.

"I'll talk to Teddy about it."

She had nothing, of course. With no regular bills to pay, the idea of having to make regular payments for anything remained foreign to her. She hadn't thought about the loan since she got the $2,000. She spent any money she made on movies, drinks, dinner, and clothing.

It bothered her. So one night, as they did some coke in his office, she asked Teddy about it. How could she pay off Natty?

"I have an idea," he said. "There's a little thing I want you to do for me. I've got a cowboy coming in who can spend a lot of money. Big tipper, too. Can you just be sure he's having a good time? Give him a little of that Wendy love?"

"Of course, Teddy," she said. "And this will help pay off that loan a little?"

"Definitely," he said and gave her a big hug. "You're the best."

Minutes later, she watched Teddy walk with his arm around the shoulders of a middle-aged man in a cowboy hat, bolo tie, and a mid-sized paunch that ledged over a silver belt buckle of Texas with horns. His long black sideburns belied his bald top, revealed when he took off his hat to greet Wendy with a "Ma'am."

For the next two or three hours they had free drinks, made small talk, and laughed as the Texan meandered from blackjack to poker to craps to roulette. She learned all about his construction work with oil companies. He got bits and pieces of her—that Mary Ann from "Gilligan's Island" visited her fourth-grade class, how she used to tie up her horse at the Caesars Palace fountain, and that her mom worked in secrecy at the Test Site.

"And what about you, little girl?" Texas asked. "What do you do?"

Make bushels of money for Teddy, she thought.

"You know, I just want Vegas to be as friendly to Texans as Texas is to Las Vegans," she said, smiling. She winked and drawled in her best "Beverly Hillbillies" impression: Y'all come back now, hear?

Teddy walked up mid-laugh.

"Ya' got a good one here, Teddy, yessiree," Texas said, red-faced.

"Wendy's as good as they come," Teddy said.

Way past midnight, Wendy was about to turn into an old hag without her beauty sleep. As she hugged Texas goodbye, Teddy made a suggestion.

"Wendy, why don't you see that this good ol' boy is able to find his room, will ya'?"

"Yeah," Texas snickered. He squeezed Wendy tight around the waist. "I might get lost."

Wendy flashed a look at Teddy.

"He needs some of that Wendy love," Teddy said, slapping his back. "He's had a long day."

Texas held her waist tight as he walked the seventeen-year-old to the elevator up to his suite.

As soon as Texas started to snore, Wendy dressed herself. Head down to avoid anyone of her co-workers' eyes, she walked to the casino's side door and took a cab to her apartment.

❖ ❖ ❖

Months passed, and the December of what would have been Wendy's senior year at Western High School arrived. Las Vegas hated December. Though casino owners and plenty of those in the Outfit in the Midwest collecting the casino skim considered themselves religious, God and Christianity and Christmas trees and the selflessness of gift buying for others played on people's minds. It didn't exactly mesh with the "Sin City" image that Las Vegas nurtured.

Teddy had a plan. He sent Wendy in a black stretch limousine to the Dunes, the Sands, the Flamingo, the Algiers, and any other Strip casino where "his" gamblers had been spotted throwing down money and stacking chips. Coax them back here, he told her, and pretty soon you won't owe us a thing.

It worked, because men liked Wendy. When she looked men in the eye, her unexpected gaze and kind smile threw them off their guard. Some blushed. Others saw in her eyes the truth—more bashful than unattainable, more insecure than confident, more girl than woman. She held an innocence rarely seen in Las Vegas, least of all from a casino emissary. But she was also a Binion Girl. Someone that beautiful could be theirs if they wanted her.

❖ ❖ ❖

Wendy didn't gamble seriously. When Teddy sent her to other casinos with money to gamble, it was just as a prop so she could sit at the tables next to the men. Men, she knew, but only in the way of a young woman who had them forced upon her. She treated them with deference and respect, even if it repulsed her to do so.

She let them do most of the talking. She let them feel in charge. And she liked best that she did her job well, which made Teddy happy, which meant he rarely asked her to shell out "that Wendy love."

Sometimes they took it even without Teddy's say-so.

Wendy found Vincent fidgeting with chips at a Dunes poker table. She sidled up to him. And he won the hand. Gamblers loved Wendy's presence; they seemed to win more.

"Come on back to the Horseshoe," she said. "Teddy and everybody else misses you."

"They miss me losing," he chuckled, then turned to her. "Tell you what, you sit by me and I'll go with you."

"That's what I do," Wendy laughed.

When they got up to leave, Vincent convinced Wendy to let him give her a ride. Normally, a Horseshoe limousine picked up her and the client. But she wasn't worried. Vincent seemed nice enough.

But on the way, he said he had to take a detour to his apartment a few blocks east of Las Vegas Boulevard to pick up some money. Wendy went in with him because she had to use the bathroom.

"There's one in my bedroom," Vincent said. His roommate slept on a couch in the living room.

Red shag carpeting covered the floor and black-light posters of lions and spirals and Pink Floyd decorated the wood-paneled walls. He had a waterbed with an ornate Asian tiger woven into the bed cover. The sink faucet looked spit-shined and the towels hung in perfect order on a rack by the shower. Felt like a hotel, Wendy smiled to herself, wondering at the relationship between the two "roommates."

She opened the door to find Vincent locking the bedroom door.

"We're not going back yet."

He walked up to her, pulled her hair, and jammed his hand into her crotch.

"Stop it!"

He smashed his fist into her cheekbone, picked her up, and threw her on the bed. He got on top of her and pinned her arms at her side with his knees. When he started to unzip his jeans in front of her face, she thrust her hips and threw him off balance. He grabbed her by the hair and dragged her across the floor.

"I'll kill you if you say another fucking word."

When he got up after finishing, Wendy quickly pulled up her panties. She saw his roommate standing just outside the bedroom.

"Hey," Vincent said, breathing hard. He chuckled. "Why don't you get a little something, too?"

"Thank you, Vincent," the other man said. "It'll be my pleasure."

❖ ❖ ❖

When she walked out of the bedroom, the men were drinking beers and staring at her. Vincent put down his beer and stood up. He stood with a cat's stillness, barely breathing. If he thought she would tell anyone, he'd kill her right then. Instinct took over and Wendy calmed herself. She managed to smile and shook her head and looked at them as two mischievous boys caught with extra cookies.

"Guys, I'm really tired, so I better get back to the casino and call it a night."

Vincent sat back down and she walked out the door.

She was a block away when she started to sob. Finding a pay phone, she called the casino, screaming for Teddy. A limousine picked her up, and by the time it got to the

Horseshoe, she had run the rape through her mind over and over. She was hysterical.

This time, waitresses, security guards, dealers, and pit bosses gathered around to comfort her, and they didn't hold back their rage.

"Teddy you've got to do something!" a security guard implored. "How can you let this happen to her? This is wrong."

"Everybody calm down," Teddy said. "I'll take care of it."

Wendy never saw Vincent in the Horseshoe again. If Teddy had someone kill him, it would have been justice in her eyes. Deep down, she knew he did nothing, and she called him a "coward" behind his back. And at long last, she constructed the emotional shell that the rest of America expects from everyone who lives in a city dominated by a singular ethos: money at all costs.

For the next year, Wendy smiled at the right times, slept with whomever when ordered. She had barely a thought for her family. "Mom" was a distant concept that barely dented Wendy's shield. She could see that woman's face in her mind's eye and feel nothing.

Wendy's hardening meant opportunity for Teddy. Lack of emotion implied she had become a vault—close-mouthed and reliable. He needed that in someone he was going to have flying to and from the Midwest a handful of times each year to deliver and return suitcases of money. All she had to do was keep her mouth shut and do what she was asked to do. He called it "the Outfit."

The trips, the sex, even the Kansas City mobster who proposed—none of it felt real, as if she looked down and watched herself from a perch on a cloud, as if Teddy's "stringy-haired little girl" were an actor she followed on

TV. Disembodied. Pain free. She saw Point B and got there from Point A.

Close to Thanksgiving of 1974, Wendy heard the first knock on the door of her downtown apartment on a Saturday morning. She opened the door to her older sister, Anne.

"Wendy, it's time to come home."

Wendy tried to close the door but Anne caught it, forced it open, and stepped inside. "Do you know how long it took us to find you?" she said.

Her eyes welling with tears, Wendy ran through a litany of reasons she couldn't go home—she owed money, she had a job, she wasn't the same person who could just live with her parents anymore, Dad was right about her being a whore, and, most of all, the single hurdle she would never get over was that she had shamed not just herself but her mom. Her mom who never drank or smoked, who stood by a husband even when she had every right to leave him.

"I can't face her," Wendy said. "I can barely look at myself in the mirror."

"I don't care," her sister said. "We love you and you're coming home. I'm not leaving without you."

They drove home in the same car Wendy had jumped from some three years earlier. Jumping out crossed her mind again. This time, she simply had no will. Any personal barriers constructed over the years had been crushed in the last year. Mom's tears? Dad's scorn? She deserved it. Nowhere on Earth was far enough to outrun the self-loathing she felt every waking moment.

When Wendy walked through the front door, Patricia Watson fell to her knees crying. Her dad looked at her from the couch with tears in his eyes. Wendy stared for a full minute. She walked to her mom and knelt. Then put her arms around her. Her dad got up and hugged them both.

In the almost three years since Wendy had left home, little had changed in the Watson household, beyond the fact that Michael either lived in jail or flopped with people who didn't mind or shared in his addiction to shooting pool.

Within days, Wendy's mom helped her enroll in Clark County Community College, which had recently opened. Wendy had a quick mind that always did well with numbers. Why not accounting, her mother said. "Just try something different—if it doesn't work, try something else."

She told admissions she had a G.E.D., though she didn't. They let her enroll and she took classes in accounting.

Problem was, Wendy barely had gotten into her first class when the phone began to ring. First it was Teddy. Then the bellmen. Then the poker players and gamblers. On and on. Teddy begged her to return, said she had made such a personal impact on him and everyone at the Horseshoe that the place just wasn't the same without her.

"Don't say no, just think about it," he pleaded.

Wendy knew why he kept calling. Her personal stories of rape and abandonment in a Texas brothel; her being under eighteen and working at the casino at all hours. Even if the state's Gaming Commission ignored it because, after all, it was the Horseshoe, Las Vegas was still Mayberry. People talked. People wouldn't like it if the Horseshoe, a place more entwined with the fabric of the city than the shared agony of baking summer nights, had done something to hurt one of their own. More than that, Wendy knew names, addresses, and stories of her cash deliveries to and from the Midwest. The kind of information that could make a federal agent's career and force the Gaming Commission to revoke the Horseshoe's license. Wendy knew what Old Man Binion would do if the casino ever went under: "He'd kill Teddy."

The risks were huge. Teddy needed her back in the circle, back under his control. Wendy, meanwhile, was just beginning to feel slightly in control, although she was haunted day and night by memories. The poker-playing rapists visited her dreams. A few moments of silence gave the pigs in Texas with their smell and grime entry to her mind.

School wasn't a remedy, however. Being among all those "goodie-two-shoes" students and instructors somehow made her feel even dirtier and full of guilt. She definitely didn't belong there.

Fuck them all. She called Teddy.

"I'll come back, but I want a real job," she said, talking from a pay phone on campus. "No more late nights, no more hanging with the gamblers. A real job, real hours."

He had just the job. She paused, which he took as encouragement, so he launched into a long history of this great guy, an old family friend. He didn't even work in the casino, but needed a secretary. "Tom Hanley," Teddy told her. "He's a longtime union man in town. And he's as real as it gets."

CHAPTER SEVEN

It wasn't his smile, because he rarely broke from a natural frown. It wasn't anything spiritual or an aural glow, though Wendy had seen auras emanate from other people since childhood.

Tom Hanley had this: When he walked through the Horseshoe, people either put their heads down and got out of his way, or they went out of their way to greet him with a smile, a handshake, or the kind of pleasantry normally reserved for high-rollers—men with lots of money the casino wanted to take.

Far from polished, Hanley never dressed up but he was meticulously clean. His shirt was always a starched, cloud-white, button-down dress shirt, with a brilliant white T-shirt underneath. Over these he wore jean coveralls that he'd never wear if they showed a hint of grime. He carried his dad's gold, antique pocket watch on a gold chain, one of about a hundred gold watches he had collected over the years. His boots were Red Wings, custom made to accommodate his abnormally high arches.

He always had a pistol hidden from view in a pocket. Though simply dressed, he carried himself with a ramrod sense of superiority, head held high, and with such ease and certain sense of ownership of the space around him. People who didn't know him, but heard everyone address him as "Mr. Tom," were mystified. The "big shot" treatment didn't jibe with the clothes.

When Wendy got to the Horseshoe, she noticed a dis-
tinguished-looking older man in front of the hostess table.
She walked up to him and he looked down at her.

"Are you Mr. Tom Hanley?" she asked, looking up.

"Yes I am, young lady. What's left of him," he cracked.

And a thing happened that caught her off guard. As he
locked his cold, blue eyes to hers, she caught his aura in
her peripheral vision. It was black, the darkest black, the
black of coal, coffee-grounds black, the black of the deep
desert on a moonless night when your hand disappears in
front of your face, the enclosing black of a lightless basement. She held her breath and looked down as he shook
her hand. When she looked back up, the black was gone.
Now it was white. She could breathe again and smile.

Wendy's mom used to say her little girl had such good
intuition that she could see things before they happened
and maneuver to keep out of danger. Maybe too eager to
get out of Binion's, she ignored the dark and focused on
the light.

When they sat down for breakfast in the café, she
consciously decided not to look at him as he tossed his
plate toward the waitress because his eggs weren't runny
enough. "Do them right," he snarled.

She let it pass. When she looked up again, he was smiling. They talked about how Teddy wanted her to have a
good, honest job.

"I still have school," Wendy said.

"No problem," Tom replied, knowing well that school
would be out of the picture soon enough. He just had to
give it time.

He finished his plate, pushed back from table, and
looked at Wendy with a smile that exuded kindness.

"I would love to have you come and work for me," he said. "I need someone like you."

Wendy was flattered. She didn't read the local papers. She had no idea who he was beyond that the Binions seemed to fear him, the employees respected him—and he wanted *her*.

They talked for hours more about the Binions, the Horseshoe, growing up in Las Vegas, Red, her brother's troubles, her mom's job at the Test Site. Tom listened to every word, caught every vocal inflection, took note of which stories caused her the most pain and the most happiness. When he was certain she was done, he told a bit about himself, of moving to Texas, Colorado, and Las Vegas. He and Benny were long and close friends. "I'm a union man," he stated proudly.

A widower and father, he had lived in Las Vegas for twenty-five years, and he fought the good fight as a union leader, blue-collar workers banded together to better their lot. In spinning his personal history, Hanley left out details that most people who read the local papers already knew. Union riots. Resisting police. Murder accusations. The story of his son found passed out from a heroin overdose. By the mid-'60s, his dangerous persona was well known to the editor of the *Las Vegas Sun*, Hank Greenspun, who wasn't afraid to write about Hanley's checkered past.

Tom would one day tell Wendy about approaching Greenspun and calling him a "Christ-killing son of a bitch." That led to a Greenspun editorial in which he compared Tom to Hitler.

Hanley got his revenge, however. In 1963, he told Wendy, he torched the offices of the *Las Vegas Sun*, causing about $1.5 million in damage. And though he was suspected of doing it, he was never charged. He said he did it while Greenspun was on a trip to Switzerland.

"I knew he could do nothing about it, because he was clear across the ocean," Tom told her. "I wanted him to feel like I did when I could do nothing about the slander he wrote about me. On top of that, I ruined his vacation! He got the message. Next time, I would kill him."

Hanley's power in Las Vegas was such that he later succeeded in signing the first union contract on behalf of Las Vegas casino dealers. The union fell apart when Hanley was sentenced to a year in jail for interfering with an IRS agent who turned up at his office to question him about his income tax returns.

So numerous were the allegations against Hanley, and so notorious was his life, that an article in May 1968 about a lawsuit against him for libel tried to squeeze all the pending allegations against him into one quick paragraph: "Among other Hanley cases currently in the courts: extortion charges by Diamond Jim's Nevada club; attempted murder, robbery and kidnapping and robbery charges in connection with the alleged attempt on the life of a former Hanley aide; and robbery and assault and battery charges stemming from the beating of a sheet metal shop owner ..."

What he could never tell her, but what she would only understand by witnessing it, was that Tom Hanley saw the world as not too different from one of the machines he so expertly took apart and rebuilt. Connect this wire to this gizmo and it works. Cut the wire, and it dies. Yes or no. Black or white. Life or death. People lived, and Hanley sometimes got to kill those chosen to die.

By the time Wendy met Tom, federal, state, and local law enforcement authorities had arrested him nineteen times in Nevada. Arrests included one allegation of murder and one attempted murder. Charges also included kidnapping, federal extortion, and a grocery list of lesser charges such as criminal libel, robbery, and resisting arrest.

"I know where you live," he told Wendy. "I can pick you up in the morning. We'll come here for breakfast and get you to work."

CHAPTER EIGHT

Tom drove to Wendy's house every morning, picked her up, and drove to the Horseshoe for breakfast. No one but a few employees wandered the place at eight a.m. Tom never had to be anywhere. The two would sit for hours talking and drinking coffee. After a few hours at the shop, they'd return to the Horseshoe for lunch.

She logged receipts and payments, which amounted to all of a few pen strokes each week, because Tom had very little business. Few people called for service. As for those who did call, unless they were old ladies or single moms, he wouldn't take their business. For them he'd not only fix their swamp cooler or furnace, he'd do it for free.

"Some people need help in this world," he'd say.

With little money coming in, Wendy figured the place stayed open because of its low overhead. The office was a trailer located just north of downtown Las Vegas, far from homes and retailers. Tough desert weeds hid the trailer's sharp edges.

Other calls came from union officials, or Benny Binion, or attorney Harry Claiborne. Sometimes men in Chicago or Kansas City were on the line. Wendy spent her time alphabetizing the business files in a gray metal cabinet. She cleaned a lot. Benny Binion gave her a horse, a direct descendant of one of his quarterhorses, that she could ride around in the desert behind the shop. They had chickens in a pen that she fed every day.

Noontime trips to the Horseshoe for lunch relieved the boredom. All smiles and winks and "how's my stringy-haired little girl?" Teddy kissed her cheek and made sure they had the hidden booth in the back corner of the restaurant.

About a week after Wendy started her job, Natty hurried to their table.

"Mr. Hanley, how are you and the beautiful Wendy?" Natty chattered.

"Doing great, Natty," Tom said. "What can we do for you?"

"Nothing, I just want to tell Wendy your loan is taken care of. Gone! Disappeared! Don't even think about it."

"You owe Natty money?" Tom asked.

"I thought I still did," Wendy replied.

"Not anymore," Natty said. "I checked it out and it's all taken care of."

"That's great, Natty," Tom said. "Anything else?"

"Nope, just want you two kids to have a great time! Great time. Nothing to worry about here. It's all taken care of."

Wendy ran it through her mind. Natty's generosity, obviously at the behest of the Binion's; a paying job for doing mostly nothing; the queenly treatment by Teddy. Her respect for Tom only grew.

He tried to kiss her the first week on the job.

❖ ❖ ❖

Spring in Las Vegas appears hot to most of the world, reaching the high eighties, but it's a relief to the desert dwellers who grow tired of the previous four months of forty-degree nights and sixty-degree days. Bright desert marigolds, baby-blanket blue buttercups, and the downy white of jimson weed bloom. Girls, as Las Vegas women seem to be called even as grandmas, shed warm clothes for those that cover just enough to make them cool in public.

Desire blossoms, too. On a perfect day in April 1975, Tom and Wendy sat chatting in the office.

"There's not much to do around here," Wendy said.

"Just having you around helps me," he answered, and then added with a chuckle, "And you do a lot around here—you do a lot of laughing. I bet you're pretty ticklish."

"Terribly," Wendy replied, laughing.

"Like this?" and he poked a finger at her waist. She yelped and jumped back.

"Don't you even think about it!" she said.

He walked toward her. She backed up. He kept coming. Then she spun away and he chased her inside the office, two second-graders laughing as they played boys-chase-girls. Then he caught her and pulled her close.

He smelled of age, of Old Spice Cologne.

Wendy pulled away. He apologized.

"I got carried away," he said, his lower lip jutting out, head hung low. "I'm sorry. An old fart like me has no business ..."

"That's okay," she said. "Let's just forget about it, pretend it never happened."

Wendy could live with that. She wanted nothing more from Tom or, really, any men. Her experiences in Texas and as "Teddy's girl" had emptied her of that kind of desire. She saw men only through the eyes of a victim—men who wanted to dominate and own, to denigrate even if they had to pay money to do so.

Gradually the two began to spend more time together. More and more, she stayed at his house instead of at her parents' house a few miles to the west.

Then she met Gramby when he came to the office one day. Wendy found him incredibly attractive. His prominent cheekbones were hewn from rock. His short dark hair fell wherever it wanted and irresistibly accentuated those cheeks. He had heavy, kissable lips and eyelids at half-mast, bedroom sapphires that gazed at a stranger with curiosity but, too, with pain. He said little, listened intensely, and always walked around with his hands in his pockets.

And he was dark. Nothing good emanated from him. "Dark and mean," Wendy said to herself. He didn't like her from the first.

He stood just beyond the front door, head leaning sleepily to one side, his lips pursed in a disgusted look, and he stared. He didn't care when she looked up. He kept staring.

"Can I help you?"

"I'm the son," Gramby said.

"Son of what?"

"Tom."

Gramby felt danger in her being there. She felt attracted to him.

"What are you doing here?" he asked.

"I'm Tom's secretary," she said.

"Oh yeah? Dad has a lot of work now, huh?"

He scared her. Why doesn't he like me, she thought? Did I take his job? What's going on?

"Dad's my mentor, you know," Gramby said. "He has me, too. Right there at his side."

He turned around quickly, found the doorknob, and jumped into his car, spewing dust and gravel as he sped away.

Tom moved fast. In March, she moved into his house. In November, they signed and paid for a marriage license.

The local papers printed Tom's headshot with news of the betrothal underneath.

In early 1976, the two married at a ranch in Jordan, Montana, a good twenty-hour drive from Las Vegas. Tom wore a bolero, tan cowboy hat, and boots stitched with a miniature cattle rope winding through them. Decorative brocade covered the shoulder and collarbone area of his black-checkered shirt, matching the design at the cuffs. Except for the .45 revolver tucked into the front waist of his pants, his outfit reminded Wendy of Howdy Doody.

Tom had suggested they dress up as square dancers, so "after we're married, we can do some square dancing." Wendy picked out something from a Sears & Roebuck catalogue that took seven days to arrive. She ordered a red skirt with the same mini-lassos looping through it and strips of fabric hanging from the edge, a red blouse with white brocade, and a white hat and white cowboy boots. In the mirror she giggled at the cowgirlish go-go dancer looking back.

She invited no one and none of Tom's relatives were invited.

When Wendy walked out of the ranch bedroom, Tom's face got bright pink. "Oh, you got red," he said of her skirt. "Wow. You're going to be full of all kinds of passions, aren't you?"

A few ranch hands stood by as witnesses as a preacher officiated. They didn't have a honeymoon.

Wendy's personal belongings consisted mostly of clothes purchased while working at the Horseshoe. She didn't consider them "work" clothes at the time, because she spent all her time at the casino. They were casino clothes, grocery-shopping clothes, go-to-the-movies clothes. Tom made her toss them all or give them to her friends.

"You're not a hooker, fer chrissakes," he said.

He bought her durable clothes—jeans, well-made blouses, a few Sunday dresses. Nothing above the knee. He cleared his stuff out of one dresser in the bedroom for her.

He took down a picture of him and Mary Lou, and got rid of any knickknacks or remembrances of his former wife. The walls were mostly barren. Mary Lou's feminine touch, if ever she lent it to the 2,600-square-foot house, had dried up years before as she lost herself in booze.

❖ ❖ ❖

Having grown up with six siblings, Wendy laid back at night in her ocean of space and quiet, moved as little as possible and listened for movement or sound of any kind. Tom barely drank and never snored. She allowed herself moments of content.

A husband who seemed to love her, even if he was a little possessive. He worked. She was secure. In a house that they owned. And she was only twenty. Her parents didn't own a house until their late thirties. Life had turned upside down, which meant hers was finally right side up. She pinched herself one night, in a one-to-one joke with herself, as Tom slept.

CHAPTER NINE

Tom introduced Wendy to all fifty of his guns during their regular Sunday afternoon target practices in the desert. Nine-millimeter handguns, .45s, a double-barreled shotgun, which almost dislocated her delicate shoulder if she didn't hold it closer to the body in the shoulder pocket. He'd screw a silencer onto a pistol and let her have a try. Silencers, which he'd get from a made guy in Phoenix, perfected the kill because they were silent and the barrel extension tended to improve accuracy.

It wasn't exactly *Murder for Dummies*. It was gentler and serious and detailed. As they reloaded and fired, Tom flooded Wendy with information known to only a handful of people in the world, techniques garnered from decades of killings.

Examples: A man knocked down from a few gunshots might look dead, but one or two more shots in the head provides insurance. Have an alibi worked out. Pay people to lie for you if needed. It's best if the body is never found, so deep, abandoned mineshafts work well. Suicide notes come in handy, and it's pretty easy to fake an accidental death with a nice display of liquor bottles and sleeping pills left near the body.

Is that how he'd do me? Wendy wondered as she fired away on Tom's weapon of choice, a .22 rifle. He pushed Wendy to the .22 more than any other weapon.

"It's the most humane way to put a person out of their

misery, because the .22 bullet doesn't explode into the head, it travels around killing the brain," he said. The small bullet has enough power to pierce the skull but not enough to get back out. More brain gets minced when the bullet ricochets "like a ball in a pinball machine."

Then he'd show her, touching the muzzle of his emptied .22 against her head. "Place the gun right there, just above the ear against the temple where the skull is thin. That will drop them," he said. "When they're down, shoot the heart at least three times. The job is done."

You don't bury them. Throw them down an abandoned mineshaft. No digging and virtually undiscoverable.

It was pragmatic, he said, because it was fast, and caused fewer problems for everyone involved.

"You see, Wendy, they are dead as soon as they hit the ground. They don't even know what hit them."

As Tom's trust in Wendy grew, he revealed more about the various hits he'd undertaken or arranged, most of them for cash, some for himself—witnesses who testified or planned to testify against him, friends filled with so much information that the threat of it spilling into police hands kept him awake at night.

"I'm not cheap," he'd boast as he held out his pistol as an extension of his arm, closed one eye and fired. "Whoever dies by this hand died because they deserved to die."

That included James Hartley.

❖ ❖ ❖

As the business agent for the Las Vegas office of the AFL's Sheet Metal Workers Union, Hartley and Hanley were friends and colleagues. Hartley's friendship with Tom could be seen in a newspaper article from 1948, after accusations arose that Tom beat up a steel metal worker in his union office. The worker didn't like that he had been taken off a job on a Sears & Roebuck store on East Fremont Street. He confronted Hanley, and Hanley savagely beat him. In late December 1948, Hartley testified in Tom's defense.

Six years later, Hartley was dead. Tom told Wendy that he had killed him following a dispute over a sheet metal union election. To emphasize his anger, Tom said that after the killing he took Hartley's car to California and parked it in front of the sheet metal union's main office in Los Angeles.

At the time, police thought they had a good lead. They found .22-caliber slugs in Hartley's body and had learned from another sheet metal worker that Hanley had recently purchased a .22 rifle with the worker's assistance. Hanley denied any involvement in the death. Police never solved the case.

Tom killed others. Some of them he knew as his best friends, including plumber's union boss Ralph Alsup.

"Hell," Tom told Wendy. "We did Hartley together. We'd been together forever."

Alsup and Hanley were indeed close. Both had a penchant for violence. In 1950, Alsup served a year in prison for shooting a member of the painters union during an argument in the labor hall. As soon as Alsup served his time, he received a state pardon. They were so close that after Alsup's murder in 1966, Tom served as a pallbearer at his funeral. He told a reporter at the funeral: "I don't know anybody closer than we were."

But by 1966 Alsup and Hanley had become rivals. Tom had some success organizing casino dealers within his American Federation of Gaming and Casino Employees. But Alsup wasn't helping, Tom told Wendy. To Tom, that meant Alsup had his own plans, plans that might interfere with Tom's desire to grow his union, and that meant Alsup had to go.

After a union meeting, Alsup stopped for some groceries, drove home, and was shotgunned as he walked through the gate to his house.

Tom said Alsup had just been diagnosed with cancer. So in reality, he was doing him a favor.

"I helped put him out of his misery," Tom said. "Do you understand? He was better off dead than to suffer from cancer."

It took two years, but by mid-1968, authorities held Tom on a murder charge, accusing him of hiring two men to kill Alsup with Tom's 12-gauge shotgun.

Police seemed to have a good lineup of witnesses who had overheard the murder arrangement being made between Tom and the killers. The only problem police had was keeping those witnesses alive.

The first to go was Marvin Shumate, a cab driver who testified that he was present when Tom paid five thousand dollars to two men in the Horseshoe casino to kill Alsup. In December 1967, Shumate's body was found at the base of Sunrise Mountain, a jagged wall of brown that protects Las Vegas's eastern flank. He had been hit from behind with a baseball bat, blasted with a shotgun, and, finally, plugged with a .38 slug behind the ear.

The second to die was Alphonse Bass, Tom's thirty-five-year-old black handyman and bodyguard. Bass also had told police he witnessed Tom giving money to two hitmen at the Horseshoe. His testimony didn't stand up long, however, against the legal might of Tom's attorney, Harry Claiborne.

Claiborne, a man with a sharp wit and infectious smile, was so well known and respected, he was appointed to a federal judgeship in 1978 by President Jimmy Carter. (In 1984, he was convicted of tax evasion, later serving seventeen months in prison. He was impeached and removed from the bench by Congress in 1986.)

He was also a trusted personal friend to Tom. (Years after the Alsup trial in 1976, Wendy and Tom made a few weekend trips to Claiborne's house to drop off envelopes full of cash, which caused Tom to complain bitterly. Tom said the money was from Joe Conforte, operator of the Mustang Ranch brothel in Northern Nevada. Conforte wanted Claiborne to spread the money around to make sure Ross Brymer, Conforte's bodyguard, didn't serve a long term in prison for killing Oscar Bonavena at the Mustang Ranch in 1976. Brymer later pleaded guilty to voluntary manslaughter of Bonavena, who had once been a top-ranked heavyweight boxing contender, and served fifteen months in prison. Conforte, who now lives in Brazil, could not be reached for comment. "I can't believe we're doing errands for that low-life scum pimp," Tom told Wendy.)

In court, Claiborne shredded Bass's testimony by holding up a twenty-two-page document, purportedly Bass's statement to a different attorney in California, in which he claimed police coerced him into testifying against Tom by threatening him with kidnapping and rape charges. Bass tried in vain to repudiate the document, but the judge tossed out his testimony as unreliable.

In December 1968, prosecutors dropped the charges against Hanley.

Three months later, firefighters found Bass's charred body in the basement of the burned-out home of Tom's sister, Jane Fitzgerald. Fitzgerald told police that Bass had asked to live there because he was broke. In fact, Tom told Wendy, Bass had come "begging" for forgiveness, so Tom let him stay with his sister, whose house was close to the air-conditioning shop.

"I wanted to trust him again," he told Wendy. "I just couldn't do it. He had to go. He died for nothing."

Tom hinted to Wendy that Gramby did the job, getting Bass into the basement while Fitzgerald was out of town, drugging him, then setting the house on fire. Bass was found tied to an expensive antique Chippendale chair. Ruining the expensive chair to kill someone infuriated Tom's sister.

"I can't believe you let that chair burn up!" she'd frequently remind Tom. "And then they left the mess for Al and me to clean!"

Investigators believed arsonists started a fire in two or three places, and toxicology tests later found the barbiturate Tuinal, a "downer," in Bass's blood. One investigator told reporters the drug "may account for the reason (he) was in the fire longer than a person would normally be."

Fitzgerald and Tom's personal, live-in attorney Al Dreyer were initially accused in the killing. They both had alibis, however, and the allegations went nowhere in court.

❖ ❖ ❖

"That's how it is out here," Tom said, repositioning the .22 rifle and prying Wendy's fingers from the trigger and barrel so she could get a better grip, firm but not too tight.

In just one year, 1968, he had been arrested four times. Once for attempted murder and kidnapping; once for extortion; another time for conspiracy to commit robbery and robbery; and the last for Alsup's murder. Each time, he was allowed to surrender at the time of his choosing. And he was never convicted in any of the crimes. He retold the stories with no small measure of pride, as examples of his intellectual dominance over police, over attorneys, over anyone who ever tried to outsmart him.

He allowed himself moments of pride with Wendy, taking ownership of the Hartley, Alsup, Bass, and Shumate killings, cracking a smile at the attempts by authorities to pin charges on him.

Wendy just loaded her gun and fired. She never uttered a word of astonishment, rarely offered an opinion. Tom terrified her. She watched her every move, thought out every word before she spoke. Opinions can be said to mean one thing but mean something entirely different to the listener. She couldn't take that kind of risk with a man like Tom, who not only admitted to having one of his closest friends killed, but dared to kill the former chief of the FBI's Las Vegas office.

CHAPTER TEN

Tom took credit for Al Dreyer's death, too. Having lived under Tom's roof for more than a decade, Dreyer and Tom had developed a relationship that might be called symbiotic by only the most sadistic of sociologists.

Dreyer did so much legal work for Hanley that the newspapers described him as Hanley's "personal attorney." He wasn't paid for billable hours, however, but with free room, board, and the occasional taste of whiskey, a treat Hanley kept under strict control. Dreyer was an alcoholic. And as Hanley did with his wife, Mary Lou, he went around town and forbade casinos and taverns from serving the lawyer alcohol. But it wasn't because Hanley wanted Dreyer to remain sober.

Like Mary Lou, Dreyer had a shot glass that he clung to every night when Tom came home, waiting for a pour of whiskey. It worked like this: Tom let Dreyer have a few shots at the Ogden Street home but nowhere else in town—and Dreyer worked overtime filing suit after suit, many of them frivolous, alleging libel against newspapers that wrote negative stories about Tom.

Eventually, Dreyer knew too much about Tom's activities. He was a longtime friend and a great legal mind, but he had to go. Tom said that when Dreyer went into a local hospital for routine surgery, he made arrangements to make sure he left in a hearse. (The surgeon has since died,

and no formal allegations of wrongdoing by him were ever
filed with local authorities.)

Dreyer was dead, but it was curious to Wendy that Tom
never seemed to be able to shut him or many others out
of his mind. Whenever he went into the back of the shop,
or into the backyard to work on some machinery, Tom's
animated talks with the deceased made Wendy shiver up
and down her spine. He carried on with Dreyer, Bass,
Alsup, and others as though they were standing before
him in the flesh.

"Al, Al, goddammit, you know I had to do it! Your drinking and the police wanting to talk to you, I had no choice."

From what she could hear, the dead were trying to tell
Tom he didn't have to kill them, that they never would
have talked. Tom always had a pat answer: "Well, you're
dead now, so I don't have to worry about it!"

One ghost who never showed up in the backyard was
that of William Coulthard.

Coulthard was a different kind of target. He wasn't one
of Tom's lackeys, wasn't a casino hanger-on, and wouldn't
be easily plied or influenced by money.

He had integrity. And wealth. His murder put an indel-
ible stain on Las Vegas, solidifying its reputation as a mob
stronghold where police would rather look the other way
than get involved.

In Las Vegas law enforcement and legal circles, Coulthard
was royalty. In the 1940s, he became the first resident agent
for the FBI in Southern Nevada. Then he earned a law
degree after leaving the FBI in 1945. In the early '50s, he
was elected to the state Assembly, where he served twice
as speaker pro tem. He became a deputy city attorney and

later went into private practice, at one point serving as president of the Nevada Bar Association.

In 1948, he even testified in court against Hanley in the case of the beaten sheet metal worker.

Coulthard became fairly wealthy in private practice, with banking interests as clients. He also wed into money. In the early '40s, he married Lena Silvagni, whose father had built the Hotel Apache on Fremont Street. Later, it became the Horseshoe. In 1955, Silvagni, just forty-two, died after heart surgery in a Los Angeles hospital.

As Silvagni's heir, Coulthard held onto his thirty-seven percent ownership of the land upon which the Horseshoe stood. In 1972, that ownership started to give Benny Binion a migraine. Binion wanted to own the land beneath his casino. Coulthard didn't want to sell it to him. Indeed, in *The Money and the Power*, the authors contend that Coulthard had negotiated the sale of the land to one of Binion's competitors.

"That son of a bitch was trying to extort Old Man Binion," Tom said. "Benny wouldn't have it. He tried to negotiate with the asshole, but the son of a bitch wouldn't budge. So he had to go. We blew the son of a bitch up."

It was more than the Las Vegas casino kingpin could stomach.

On July 25, 1972, Coulthard stepped into his Cadillac parked in the garage of the Bank of Nevada building at 300 S. Third Street. Key in the ignition, he turned it and detonated dynamite affixed to the car's undercarriage. The explosion severed his head. Another twenty vehicles were damaged.

Afterward, the Binions signed a one hundred-year lease with Silvagni's brothers, the remaining owners of the land.

Wendy was sitting with gamblers at Binion's at the time and hadn't yet met Tom. But they all heard the explosion, and the casino was alive with talk and laughter, with people giggling about it.

Even with police and federal agents all over the case, the investigation faltered, then went cold. No one was ever charged.

After Wendy became part of the family, Gramby bragged one night about putting the bombs under Coulthard's Cadillac.

"That sucker almost blew off the lid of the parking lot," he said. The name rang a bell, because when she was doing Teddy's bidding at the Horseshoe, Wendy remembered the gallows humor among the poker players the night of the explosion, which everyone in the casino heard and felt. The players were somber that night, kind of sad, until someone blurted out: "Boy, they must have shot him to the moon."

A few chuckles later and they were all back to normal, back to the business of poker.

Tom rarely found humor in the bombing because it dogged him for years. Lt. Beecher Avants, who led the Coulthard investigation for Las Vegas Metro's homicide unit, brought it up whenever he saw Tom.

"I'm going to get you for the Coulthard murder," he would yell at Tom. "I know you did it."

Avants couldn't "get" Hanley, of course, without the say-so of Sheriff Ralph Lamb, a man who willingly accepted loans from the Binions for the department's "undercover" operations. "That son of a bitch is always breathing down my neck," Tom grumbled.

Avants later told the *Las Vegas Sun* that he approached

federal authorities with information in 1977 linking Tom and Gramby to the Coulthard bombing. A gardener had identified the Hanleys, Avants said, at Coulthard's house on the morning of the murder.

The Feds didn't seem interested. By that time, they had started working with Tom and Gramby, both under arrest for the murder of Al Bramlet, in an attempt to uncover underhanded dealings of the unions with casinos.

"They were reluctant," Avants told the *Sun*.

Four years after Coulthard died, in June 1976, Don Bolles, an investigative reporter who spent years exposing mob connections in Phoenix, died after six sticks of dynamite attached with magnets to the underside of his Datsun were detonated remotely.

Bolles's investigations had touched the operations of Emprise, a Buffalo, New York-based concessions company that as far back as 1958 had helped Morris "Moe" Dalitz buy the Stardust casino in Las Vegas. In 1972, Bolles testified before a House Select Committee on Crime that held hearings on Emprise's connections to organized crime. A few weeks earlier, a federal grand jury accused Emprise of trying to conceal its ownership, and the ownership of two mobsters, in Las Vegas's Frontier hotel-casino.

After an investigation, three men with no ties to the company were charged with the murder.

When Tom mentioned the Bolles bombing at home, he did it as a threat, as in, "If Greenspun doesn't watch out, he'll get what that Arizona reporter got."

Las Vegas seemed to be the epicenter of bombings for a few years in the early '70s, and all or most of them were tied to the Hanleys. In January 1976, David's Place, a non-union restaurant, was blown up on West Charleston

Boulevard. A year later, two bombs were found and disabled on the same night at the Starboard Tack restaurant and the Village Pub supper club, both embroiled in disputes with the Culinary Union. Three years later, Tom and Gramby pleaded guilty to the two bombing attempts, as well as the bombing of David's Place.

They were also thought to be involved in the bombing of the Alpine Village restaurant in December 1975, when two bombs on the roof went off thirty seconds apart with four hundred customers inside. No one was hurt. For twenty years, the restaurant had been picketed by the Culinary Union for its refusal to unionize. Tom's version was that investigators dropped any charges related to the Alpine Village bombing if Tom and Gramby pleaded guilty to the other bombings.

Deadly bombings, shotgun murders, .22s, and tossing people down mine shafts. When you're in the middle of it all, you develop the thousand-yard stare, you join in, or you find something else to focus on. Wendy focused on her daughter. She focused so hard on her daughter's every move, her beautiful tiny hands and pretty face, that she thought she could block out the chaos, all this talk of death.

There were two dead men she had a hard time forgetting, though.

Once, while in Los Angeles with Tom, she had met Jimmy Hoffa for lunch at the airport. Her mom had met the other man at the Nevada Test Site. Many years later, Patricia Watson showed Wendy the black-and-white photo taken of her with that handsome young man, John F. Kennedy.

CHAPTER ELEVEN

In the '70s, everyone believed Lee Harvey Oswald had assassinated President John F. Kennedy in 1963. But as time passed and suspicions grew, that certainty fell apart.

Libraries of books about subsequent investigations and theories have long since shattered many Americans' faith in the "truth" as laid out in the Warren Commission report on the JFK assassination.

Could Tom Hanley of Las Vegas have been somehow involved?

Just eight years old when Kennedy died, Wendy was like many Americans young and old: stunned. Not because the eight-year-old held an affinity for the man in the White House. For her it was enough to see her teacher weep openly in class, then to see her mom do the same at home, to know that something very bad had happened.

Flash forward twelve years, and how do you take it when your husband, by now known to you as a killer-for-hire, says he was part of the assassination plot, one of perhaps two or three teams hired by "the mob" to kill the president? How do you think straight when his son, Gramby, proclaims while under the spell of his own personal truth serum, heroin, that Tom was part of the "hit"?

Or how about the time Tom pulled a black pinstriped suit out of the closet, brushed off some lint, and held it up for Wendy to see.

"Did you know, Winnerferd, the one time I wore this

suit, I brought home $60,000 in cash for the Kennedy job," he marveled. "Pretty soon, I'll be bringing home another $60,000 or even $100,000 in the same suit. Let's drop it off at the cleaners."

Federal investigators appeared to just skim the surface of Las Vegas when they investigated the assassination. They came to look into Jack Ruby—who shot and killed Oswald before he could testify—and whether Ruby had been seen in Vegas.

Everyone, too, knew that Benny Binion was a reputed mobster who "ran" Dallas before moving to Las Vegas in the '40s. The guy knew that Texas city and its denizens inside and out.

But did Benny know Jack Ruby, the Dallas club owner and underworld figure who killed Oswald?

The National Archives JFK Assassination Records Collection contains more than one hundred references to Benny Binion—Lester Benjamin Binion. In 1964, the year after Kennedy's death, he is referred to in various capacities nineteen times. In one note from November 30, eight days after the shooting, federal agents talked to casino owner Jackie Gaughan, who told them he was at a rodeo with Binion two days after Kennedy was shot.

Gaughan said neither of them knew Ruby, but someone had mentioned that Ruby had stayed at the Sahara Hotel one week earlier. The next day, the Feds questioned ten more people, including pit bosses and other low-level workers, for any memory of Ruby being in their casino.

The Warren Commission summed up its findings by rejecting the idea that Ruby had been in Las Vegas. In 1979, however, the House Select Committee on Assassinations came to a different conclusion, citing "credible evidence" that Ruby had been in Las Vegas before the shooting.

So?

They wanted to know if Ruby had been in Las Vegas for instruction, or payment, or anything else that might have prompted him to shoot Oswald. Were there Las Vegas connections to the assassination?

And there was this: Dallas officers detained "three tramps" who were found, reports said, in a boxcar west of the grassy knoll on Dealey Plaza where Kennedy died. In 1992, more than thirty years later, the Dallas Police Department released what it said are the true identities of the three: Gus Abrams, John F. Gedney, and Harold Doyle.

But many years before that revelation, during one of their Sunday morning instructional shooting trips into the desert, Tom told Wendy that when he went to Dallas for the job, he dressed like a "tramp." The FBI even flew to Las Vegas to talk to him about the Kennedy job, he chuckled.

"Can you imagine, Winnerferd, they accused me of being dressed like a tramp with a rifle behind a tree?"

She looked at him from the corner of her eye.

"Maybe, maybe not," he smiled.

He brought up the tramps again, though, two years later in 1977 after his arrest for the murder of Culinary Union leader Al Bramlet. During a jail visit, Tom held up a note to Robert Peoples to go dig up Bramlet's buried jewelry because he wanted it to taken to Reno to throw off investigators. Before they left, he gave Wendy one more bit of advice.

"Dress like a farm girl, so no one recognizes you if you're stopped," he said. "That's what we did in Dallas when we dressed as tramps."

Wendy forgot about the conversation for decades. Then, while watching a television show that mentioned the three men in Dallas, she hurriedly typed "three tramps" into Google. She got chills, because the third man in one picture reminded her so much of Tom.

The black-and-white photos, however, were not a state secret. Maybe Tom had seen the same photo years earlier, or at least heard of the "tramps," and tried to use them to his advantage. How easy would it be, after all, to ensure Wendy's silence by claiming to have taken part in the most famous assassination of our time and not been caught? If he could do that, surely he could take care of her with ease, even from the confines of a jail cell.

Gramby's claim to have killed Hoffa is equally difficult to prove.

In the summer of 1975, Wendy began to feel she'd been through the grinder and still come out intact. She'd found some happiness. She had a job, she was nineteen and away from school, and she had a man in her life, albeit one much older. The true nature of Tom's work gradually dawned on her, but it was almost too much to consider—thinking about it would make her feel obligated to get out. But she couldn't run. Tom would either kill her in the attempt, or she'd end up back at the Horseshoe following Teddy's orders to sleep with gamblers and running money back and forth from Kansas and Chicago. Try as she might to ignore Tom's "work," it was Tom himself who wouldn't let her forget.

In the few months since Mary Lou Hanley's death, Tom took Wendy everywhere—indeed, he wouldn't let her out of his sight. So, when Tom had a lunch meeting with Hoffa at Los Angeles International Airport a few weeks before Hoffa disappeared, she came along.

She liked Hoffa immediately. He smiled easily, had manners enough to stand when she got up from the table to visit the ladies' room, and had a blue-collar earthiness that seemed miles away from his place as a national figurehead for the Teamsters Union.

Hoffa's name came up again months later. He was reported missing July 30. To this day, Hoffa's body has never been found. And from what Gramby and alleged accomplices contend, Hoffa will never be found.

Gramby had driven out of Las Vegas in early June and met up with Bob Jurgen and "Jackson" in Chicago. Around August 1, the three of them drove up to the house on Ogden Avenue in a brand new, fully loaded black Pontiac Grand Prix with Michigan plates.

In the house, Gramby cracked open a suitcase to show Wendy wads of cash, jewelry, and drugs. The back of the Grand Prix was packed with new clothes.

"Come on," he whispered to her. "Let's go."

Tom was behind the house digging into some machinery.

Wendy, Gramby, and the two others parked at the Horseshoe. They got a room. Wendy drank champagne as Gramby, Jurgen, and Jackson did drugs. Gramby pulled the money out of the suitcase and threw it in the air laughing, while Wendy bounced on the bed.

They couldn't believe the ease of the job for such a huge reward. All they had to do was kidnap this union official, shoot him, then got rid of the body by stuffing him into a barrel and dissolving the barrel in a huge vat of acid. When the deal was done, they were allowed to pick any car they wanted inside an automobile factory.

"And I picked out the sweetest ride they had," Jurgen boasted.

As they talked, Wendy picked up that it wasn't just a union official they had killed. They also claimed they killed Sam Giancana, former boss of the Chicago Outfit. After running afoul of the Outfit in the mid-'60s, he was replaced by Joey Aiuppa. Jackson seemed especially happy about Giancana's death. Jackson grew up on Chicago's South Side, where he said his uncle ran the Black Mafia—until Giancana had him killed.

The only thing he was irritated about was that Gramby and Jurgen had lost the gun used to kill Giancana. "If the heat find the gun, it could come back on me and I'll be sent to the big house," he complained.

With drugs enough for a week, however, the three quickly lost track of time and complaint. They didn't get past day two. The door flew open and Jurgen ran into the room.

"Tom's coming!" he yelled. "Tom's coming! What are we going to do with Wendy?"

Addled from the drugs, Gramby and Jurgen hid in the bathtub behind the shower curtain. Then they heard Tom bashing the outer door with the butt of his gun.

"You sons of bitches, where's Wendy?" he yelled.

"Wendy, you gotta go!" Jurgen yelled from the bathroom.

A deal was struck through the closed door: If Tom wouldn't come in and kill them, he could take Wendy.

Deal.

In the pickup truck on the way home, Tom didn't look angry. More forlorn and lost. He reminded Wendy that he lost a son in 1961 to a drug overdose.

"I hope you're happy with yourself," he said.

Two days later, Gramby and Jurgen came to the house

without Jackson. Both high, they ate a bit and settled onto couches in the living room. They talked and giggled as Jurgen relived a recent killing, how he had taken a large television and dropped it on someone's head.

"Gramby, did you see the head pop?" he asked. "Boom!"

"Yeah, good thing we had him pumped up and singing that blue magic," Gramby said. "He didn't feel a thing."

"Would you two drug addict sons-a-bitches shut up?!" Tom yelled.

"But Uncle Tom," Jurgen said. "It was so cool. The guy didn't even know what hit him."

Wendy got the feeling that "the guy" was Jackson.

Tom took Wendy outside and said he wanted to go for a ride. They stopped at a bar on Maryland Parkway. Wendy waited in the truck. Tom went inside and came out a bit later with Tony Spilotro. The two were yelling at each other.

"That little punk is stealing from the wrong person!" Tom spat as he got back into the truck. "Mr. Aiuppa wants his money back. I swear I'm going to run that little punk out of my town."

Tom's headache didn't stop there. When he and Wendy got home, they found Wendy's Australian shepherd, Lobo, with a huge gash in its head. Jergen walked up to Tom, got in his face, and demanded money.

"Where's my money? I did the job. All I want is my money!"

"What son of a bitch did this to Wendy's dog?" Tom demanded.

"I didn't do it, I didn't do it!" Gramby shouted.

"No, I did it," Jergen said. "Just like I bashed that head in today. Now where's my money?"

Tom pulled his pistol from his waistband, but Jergen dove out a window and ran away.

Gramby sat down with Lobo, cleaned the wound, and had Wendy hold the dog's skin together as Gramby taped it together.

❖ ❖ ❖

Less than one year later, after Tom and Gramby were both in custody for the murder of a different union leader, Las Vegas homicide Lt. Beecher Avants showed up at the house on Ogden Avenue. He showed Wendy a picture of an older man and asked if she could identify him.

"That's the man Tom and I met in L.A. during the summer of 1975," she said. "I think it's Jimmy Hoffa."

It wasn't the last time she would see Avants. But he never mentioned Hoffa to her again.

CHAPTER TWELVE

Although they were notorious, Tom and Gramby Hanley weren't always on the front burner of police investigations. Their names didn't even surface when Tamara Rand was murdered in San Diego in November 1975.

When Rand took four bullets to the head in the kitchen of her Mission Hills home, few in Las Vegas had even heard of her. That wasn't the story, however, in the business offices of Strip casinos, where the well-to-do San Diego investor and wife of a gynecologist had inserted herself into areas most Las Vegans had long ago taught themselves to avoid.

Two days before Rand's killing, Gramby threw clothes into a suitcase and left for a weekend trip to California. He seemed remorseful about this job. "I don't like killing women," he said. "But I'm going to Los Angeles to kill a witch."

Packing a large suitcase, he threw in a tool belt, yellow construction hat, and a worker's uniform. Cold case investigators would later tell Wendy that Rand was found in her home, which was undergoing construction.

The day after Rand's body was discovered, Gramby was arrested. He had run his car into a grape vineyard somewhere outside of San Jose, California. That day, Spilotro called the house to tell Tom about Gramby's accident and arrest.

While Spilotro was initially considered a prime suspect,

he had an indisputable alibi—he had spent most of that weekend with a Chicago FBI agent. Wendy said a cold case detective from San Diego worked with her for two years off and on but couldn't find enough evidence to pin the murder on Gramby.

Rand's murderer was never found, despite what at first appeared to be several strong leads. One of those was a connection to Las Vegas casino mogul Allen Glick.

The son of a Pittsburgh scrap-iron dealer, Glick was an intelligence officer in Vietnam, got into real estate back in the United States, and landed with Saratoga Development Corporation in San Diego in the early '70s. He saw "gold mines" in Las Vegas casinos, he would tell the *Los Angeles Times*, and helped position Saratoga and private investors to purchase the Hacienda for about $8.5 million.

Later, Glick obtained an estimated $62 million in Teamsters pension fund money to buy controlling shares of Recrion Corporation, which he renamed Argent Corp. The company owned four Las Vegas casinos in the '70s: the Stardust, Fremont, Hacienda, and Marina.

By 1977, Glick was a celebrated Las Vegan who supported the Boy Scouts and United Way. That year, the local B'nai Brith lodge named him Man of the Year.

Legal issues and civil lawsuits follow anyone in business. Argent Corporation was no different. But investigators thought they found something more than ordinary in a lawsuit that Rand had filed against Glick in January 1975. Rand claimed Glick owed her some $560,000. She had invested with Glick in California, then "was bitter that she was not included in his later Las Vegas casino ventures," the *Los Angeles Times* wrote. The FBI was contending that if Rand's case went to court, Glick would have been forced to open the financial books of his casinos. And if Glick would have had to open those books, they could reveal illicit deals.

Rand was murdered, and the lawsuit died with her.

That wasn't the end of Glick's troubles, however. In 1976, Nevada gaming officials talked openly about looking into possible embezzling from Argent casinos. They wouldn't call it "skimming," "because for that we would have to show management participated," a gaming official told the *Las Vegas Sun*.

This was also about the time that Wendy met Jay Vandermark, a former slot cheat hired by Argent to manage its slots. Who better to find problems, the thinking went, than someone who knew how to cheat the casino?

In May 1976, however, Vandermark may have wanted to be just about anywhere in the world other than the Stardust or Las Vegas. That's when Gaming Commission investigators opened an investigation into the the Stardust counting room after hearing about a potential slot-skimming operation that was funneling millions to mobsters in the Midwest. Skimming is when a portion of the slot wins are secretly "skimmed" before the money is officially counted and taxed. Investigators believed the skim to be around $7 million over an eighteen-month period. The problem for Vandermark—he was reporting that the skim only came to about $4 million.

Gaming Commission officials wanted to reach Vandermark before more dangerous characters did. Vandermark didn't want to meet anyone, so he fled. Officials believed he went to South America, never to be seen again.

Maybe he did go there. But he eventually returned to

Las Vegas, because in August he walked through the front door of Oasis Air Conditioning looking for Tom Hanley. Wendy had never seen the man before. But one glimpse and she knew she didn't like him.

CHAPTER THIRTEEN

Nervous, excitable, and smelling badly of body odor, Vandermark bolted through the front door and walked into the trailer office. With wisps of hair on top, thick black-rimmed glasses, and hearing aids, he was neither attractive nor odd-looking enough to attract notice. To Wendy, he was just another man. She only really paid attention as the front door closed and pushed a wave of air toward her, engulfing her in the man's inescapable stench.

He glared at her, exasperated at the thought of having to talk to someone like her; someone he knew didn't have the slightest chance of understanding his mind, his thoughts, and his predicament.

"I need to see Tom," he demanded.

"He's not here right now," she said.

She wrinkled her nose. He smelled *and* he was rude.

He left a card.

The malodorous man came back the next day and stepped into the back office with Tom. A few minutes later, Tom stepped out front and told Wendy that "Jay" would be staying in the trailer for a few days.

"Who is he?" she asked.

Someone Tom was beginning to wish he didn't know. The Stardust hired Vandermark in October 1974, close to the time that Glick became an instant millionaire by accepting about $100 million in Teamster loans to purchase casinos. The *Los Angeles Times* reported at the time that one of Argent Corporation's first moves was to centralize "slot machine supervision for all four (Argent) casinos ... Coins were hauled to the Stardust from the Marina and Hacienda ... and from the Fremont, then counted daily at the Stardust."

The skim happened like this: The Stardust's coin scale was calibrated to undercount by a third. "The coins thus skimmed off the top—above the official tabulation of gross winnings of the house—were hauled out of the counting room," the newspaper reported. The skim was estimated to be as much as $20,000 a day.

Vandermark had been staying in the trailer only a few days. But his overpowering odor to Wendy, who was six months pregnant, was more than she could stand in the oven-hot bake of Las Vegas in August.

"When is this guy going to leave?" Wendy complained to Tom one day.

Vandermark was in the back room of the office. "I don't like him. He's very sarcastic and disrespectful to me."

Tom stomped into Vandermark's room.

"Apologize to her for being so rude!" he demanded.

Vandermark apologized.

"And please take a shower!" Wendy implored.

"You disrespectful bitch," Vandermark hissed.

Tom grabbed him by the neck and threw him into a chair.

Exhausted, shrunken from worry, and looking much older than his fifty-two years, Vandermark begged Tom to make a phone call.

"Tom, you've got to get a hold of Mr. Aiuppa," he said. "I've got to clear my name."

"Mr. Aiuppa" was Joseph "Joey" Aiuppa, head of the Chicago Outfit. Ten years later, in 1986, Aiuppa would be convicted and sentence to twenty-eight years in prison for his part in the Stardust skimming operation.

"Jay, calm down," Tom said. "You're going to get to talk to Joey. I put a call into him and he will be calling soon."

"I'm just afraid Spilotro is going to show up here and find me!"

Tom assured him that nobody knew he was there.

The next day, the phone ran and a man said he wanted to speak to Tom.

"May I ask who is calling?" Wendy asked.

"Tell him it's Joey Aiuppa from Chicago," Aiuppa replied. "And how is the beautiful Wendy today?"

"Fine, Joey. Hold on and I will get Tom for you."

Wendy ran to get Tom. Vandermark stood still in the background listening.

"Hello, Mr. Aiuppa. I need to talk to you about Mr. Vandermark." Tom took a breath. "Mr. Vandermark did not steal all that money from the Stardust like Tony Spilotro told you."

A long pause as Aiuppa spoke, then Tom answered.

"But the guy only has one suitcase, and it's Spilotro who stole the money," Tom said. "He's trying to put the blame on Mr. Vandermark. Spilotro took the money and opened a jewelry store."

Tom listened some more, then said "Okay, Mr. Aiuppa, will do. By the way, when are you coming to Vegas? It must be cold in Chicago. Okay, we'll see you then." Then he hung up the phone.

"What did he say? Did he say everything was going to be all right?" Vandermark asked.

Tom took him outside so Wendy couldn't hear.

On the way home that night, Wendy groused again about Vandermark to Tom, who was driving.

"I'm not going back to the office until that person is gone," she said. "He's rude. I'm six months pregnant, Tom. I can't stand the smell!"

Tom looked over at her wild-eyed and snapped his fingers. "I will throw that smelly son of a bitch down a mineshaft and he's gone forever. No one talks to my wife like that! I'm sorry he talked to you like that, honey."

She chuckled and Tom calmed down. She thought he had to be joking. He couldn't kill someone just for being disrespectful. Now she started feeling sorry for the nervy, skinny guy. She prayed Tom wasn't serious.

❖ ❖ ❖

Wendy stayed at home the next day. Around midday, someone knocked on the front door. It was Joe Bonanno, head of the Bonanno crime family who lived in Tucson, Arizona. His presence gave Wendy a chill. Every time he showed up, it seemed like someone ended up dead. And he never came into the house, always waiting to talk to Tom outside.

He and Tom talked, and Bonanno left.

❖ ❖ ❖

She returned to the office two days later, after Tom said Vandermark had left.

Vandermark's stench was gone. But Wendy noticed something else just as unsettling. Something drippy and mushy was stuck to the wood paneling in the hallway by Vandermark's room.

"What's that dripping down the wall?" Wendy asked Tom.

"That's not supposed to be there," Tom said. He grabbed a towel from the bathroom and went to work on the mess.

As he wiped, the towel turned from white to bright red and brown.

She walked to her desk out front. Tom came out a bit later and Wendy saw him walking outside carrying Vandermark's suitcase in one hand and what looked like Vandermark's hearing aids, dangling from wires, in the other. He walked to the back shed and came back into the office empty-handed.

"Jay left some of his things behind," Tom said, walking into the office. "I have to take them to his son."

❖ ❖ ❖

At a sports bar at Flamingo and Paradise roads a few days later, Tom and Wendy were in their pickup when a young man walked up. Tom jumped out of the truck. Tom patted the kid on the shoulder, then handed him a wad of cash. After getting back into the pickup, Tom started to drive away when the kid ran up to the window.

"Tom, when you hear from my dad, here's a number you can reach me at," he said.

Driving away, Wendy asked what that was all about.

"That's Vandermark's kid. He's worried about his dad."

A few days later, they met Frank "Lefty" Rosenthal at Marie Callender's restaurant on Sahara Avenue. Rosenthal operated Argent's Las Vegas casinos, a job he would lose a few years later when the Gaming Commission denied him a gaming license.

No lunch this time. Each ordered a slice of Callender's famous pie. They paid the bill, and then walked to Rosenthal's Cadillac.

"I have the things we talked about in the truck," Tom said. He walked to his pickup, lifted the tarp, and pulled out Vandermark's black suitcase. Rosenthal opened his trunk and Tom put the suitcase inside.

"Take that envelope in there," Rosenthal said. Tom picked up the envelope and closed the trunk.

"Great job," Rosenthal said. "I'll be in touch."

"Yes sir, Mr. Rosenthal," Tom replied. "Not a problem at all."

CHAPTER FOURTEEN

Wendy lived with a hired killer, but that didn't mean she could tell one when she saw one.

Tony Spilotro knocked on the door of their Ogden Avenue home one day in late 1975. When she answered the door, his eyes got big.

"You must be Tom's daughter," said Spilotro, who by then had earned a Las Vegas reputation as a tough guy, the muscle enforcing the rule of law as laid down by the Chicago Outfit. He couldn't find Gramby, who lived around the corner. He and Gramby had just started a lucrative robbery operation, targeting jewelry stores.

"I'm his wife," she said.

Spilotro laughed. "Tom got a youngie!"

Tom stood a few feet behind Wendy. He pulled his pistol, stepped outside, and grabbed Spilotro by the back of the hair, sticking the gun in his mouth.

"You're going to apologize for that crack," he hissed.

With one of his massive hands, he grabbed the back of Spilotro's neck and pulled him into the doorway.

Wendy backed into the living room, certain she was about to see brains splattered on the front sidewalk. The next thing she knew, Tom put the gun's muzzle to Spilotro's temple and ordered him to his knees.

"Apologize!" Tom said. "This is my wife, Wendy."

Spilotro crawled a few feet toward Wendy, then looked up.

"For chrissake, Tom, put the gun down!" Spilotro pleaded. "I'm sorry, I'm sorry!"

"Tom, that's enough," Wendy said. "Please, Tom, stop."

"Now get the fuck out of here," Tom said.

Spilotro walked fast out the door, got into his Lincoln Continental, and spun gravel into the air as he hit the gas and sped away.

"Punk," Tom said, stuffing the gun back into his waistband.

It wasn't the last time Wendy saw the diminutive mob enforcer. Spilotro, dubbed "The Ant" by the media after a federal agent called him a "pissant," stood just five feet two. Spilotro and Gramby engaged in a year-long robbery spree, many of their heists worked out ahead of time with stores that would get reimbursed for their losses through insurance. The two became the original "Hole-in-the-Wall Gang" a few years before the newspapers or police gave a nickname to their methods, which often amounted to drilling holes through walls and safes to get to the goods.

In a house where Tom talked regularly with the spirits of men he had killed, where a body was folded into the backroom freezer, with bombs being constructed and bomb placements being mapped on blueprints, the heists became the fodder for much-needed comic relief in the Ogden Avenue home.

One that had them in stitches happened on a Sunday afternoon near the end of the summer in 1976 at a jewelry store near Sahara Avenue and Maryland Parkway. Gramby filled two canvas bags full of jewelry and gems, and got into his car. It wouldn't start.

The phone rang. Tom answered.

"Hey, want to go for a Sunday ride?" he asked Wendy.

They got into the pickup, drove south on Maryland Parkway, and pulled into a shopping mall. Gramby sat on the curb next to his car.

"I think it just needs a jump," he said, throwing the two clinking bags into Tom's pickup.

They lifted the hood, applied the jumper cables, and it started.

"See you back at the house," Gramby said.

"Yep," said Tom.

Gramby dumped the bags onto the living room floor. A pile of gold and silver bejeweled bracelets, necklaces, watches, and rings caught the light through the window and cast it like a disco ball on the walls.

"Oh my God!" Wendy said, kneeling on the floor as Tom and Gramby sorted through the loot. She put several rings on each finger, a few pounds of gold necklaces around her neck, and shielded her arms from wrist to elbow in gleaming gold and silver bracelets.

"I'm a queen!" she laughed, holding up her adorned arms. Everyone laughed.

They divided the hauls three ways among Tom, Gramby, and Spilotro, then dispersed pieces to subcontractors who helped with the little things along the way—getting police tips, talking to store owners. By early 1975, Las Vegas police had some idea of what was going on, but they still didn't have the proof needed to make arrests. That, or the sheriff didn't want them to move in.

A March 1975 "information report" addressed to the sheriff about "BURGLARY SUSPECTS" lists names and addresses of more than a dozen people "associated with Tom Hanley." The report lists what kinds of cars and trucks they drove, their home addresses, and why they are suspects. One man's vehicle was spotted "at several daytime burglaries." Two others had tried to sell stereo equipment stolen from a Fremont Street business or tools taken from construction sites.

Tom's method for getting the haul to Spilotro was deceptively simple and almost unknowable. Sitting on the street in front of the house was equipment used to heat tar that would be used to seal flat rooftops. Tom went out at night, put a bag of jewelry into the tar hopper, close the lid, and locked it. Spilotro had a key and would drive by at night, unlock it, pull out the goods, and drive away.

Police knew what was going on, or seemed to. One Las Vegas cop often came to the house to let Tom know about a departmental investigation, giving Tom time to create alibis, dump evidence, and otherwise snuff the trail leading his way.

Benny Binion, Tom's chief contractor who held sway over the police, did not have similar control over the FBI. But from what the Hanleys could see, the FBI's tactics were far from effective. They drove by Gramby's house one day howling in laughter, as four agents dressed in dark suits, thin black ties, and shiny black leather shoes one after the other jumped up as high as they could to catch a peek of Gramby's backyard.

Easy money fueled suspicions, too. Thinking he hadn't gotten his fair share, Spilotro showed up to Oasis Air Conditioning one morning demanding to see Gramby.

"He's not here," Wendy said. "I don't know where he is."

"You know, goddammit," Spilotro said. "Get him and get him out here. He owes me."

Tom stepped out from his office and asked what was going on.

"Gramby's holding out, and I want to talk to him about it," Spilotro said.

"Nobody's holding out, you greedy son of a bitch," Tom said. "Now get out of here."

"I want my money," Spilotro insisted.

Spilotro backed outside as Tom moved toward him with his gun out. Another man sat in his Lincoln Continental in the front passenger seat.

"Leave."

"I'm not leaving until …"

"You want to dance, you little punk? Then dance, you motherfucker," and Tom started shooting at Spilotro's feet, Spilotro jumping and backing up toward his car.

"You're a crazy old man!" he yelled as got into his Lincoln and drove away.

Tom turned around toward Wendy with a huge smile on his face.

"Did that scare you, my little Winnerferd?" he asked gently.

"No," Wendy said, then smiled. It was the only time she'd seen Tom shoot at someone. "But you sure made him dance."

Tom laughed, threw an arm over her shoulders, and they walked into the office.

Wendy, as an infant, watched over by her older sisters.

Wendy, two years after she met Teddy Binion.

Teddy Binion in front of Binion's Horseshoe.

A runaway child at sixteen, Wendy was unhappy but didn't think she could go home.

Las Vegas Metropolitan Police officers stand by as Culinary Union workers and supporters pass Binion's Horseshoe Casino.

Tom Hanley in 1968. Wendy would meet him a few years later, and although he was thirty-nine-years her senior, she'd become his wife.

Don Zirkle/Las Vegas Review-Journal

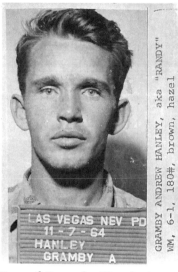

One of Gramby Hanley's many mug shots. Tom Hanley's son was bedeviled by drugs.

Tony "The Ant" Spilotro partnered with Gramby Hanley in a jewelry store heists. His violent ending was graphically depicted in the film Casino.

Al Bramlet, head of the powerful Culinary Union. His murder would eventually lead to the end of Tom and Gramby Hanley's murders-for-hire business.

Tom Hanley's wife
APR 2 6 1977 p.1 TB
surrenders to cops

By Tim Dahlberg
R-J Staff Writer

The 21-year-old wife of fugitive Thomas Hanley surrendered Monday afternoon...

Hanley's wife held
p.1 JUN 2 1977
on murder charge

By Sherman Frederick
R-J Staff Writer

Wendy Hanley, 21-year-old wife of accused killer Thomas Hanley, was arrested about 2 p.m. Wednesday on an open charge of murder in connection with the slaying of Culinary Union boss Al Bramlet, Las Vegas Metropolitan Police detectives reported.

She was arrested on the Blue Diamond Road, west of town, and was reportedly in possession of jewelry, including a watch and a ring, which allegedly belonged to Bramlet.

COMPLETE CLOSING STOCKS

Las Vegas **REVIEW-JOURNAL**

NEVADA'S LARGEST AND MOST COMPLETE NEWSPAPER

TRAILBLAZER LAS VEGAS, NEVADA, THURSDAY, JUNE 2, 1977

VOL. 69 NO. 62   PHONE 385-4241   15 CENTS   112 PAGES

Las Vegas Review-Journal Archives

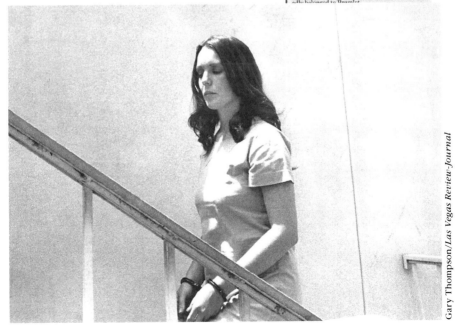

Gary Thompson/Las Vegas Review-Journal

The arrest of the young and beautiful Wendy Hanley was front page news in April and June of 1977.

Leonard Ignelzi/Las Vegas Review-Journal

Wendy's court appearances brought out the media in droves.

Benny Binion in front of the Horseshoe's million dollar display.

Wiliam Coulthard's bombed car.

Las Vegas Review-Journal Archives

Tom Hanley at the time of his arrest for Al Bramlet's murder.

Hank Greenspun, publisher of the Las Vegas Sun.

Tom Hanley claimed credit for the firebombing of the Sun's *building.*

Gary Thompson/Las Vegas Review-Journal

Allen Glick.

Las Vegas Review-Journal Archives

George Vandermark.

AP Photo/Las Vegas Review-Journal Archives

The Chicago connection. Mob boss Joseph Aiuppa.

Gary Thompson/*Las Vegas Review-Journal*

Attorney Harry Claiborne in 1976. Just two years later, President Jimmy Carter would nominate him to a Federal judgeship. The FBI would target him as a corrupt judge and he was impeached in 1986.

Harry Claiborne, Oscar Goodman, Lefty Rosenthal, Allen Glick 1976.

Gary Thompson/*Las Vegas Review-Journal*

Gary Thompson/*Las Vegas Review-Journal*

*Frank "Lefty"
Rosenthal played
a prominent role
in the Las Vegas
gambling scene.*

Jim Decker/*Las Vegas Review-Journal*

Wendy's tumultuous young life left her with
nightmares, but today she lives a outwardly serene life
in the suburbs, surrounded by a loving family.

CHAPTER FIFTEEN

Raised in Northern Nevada, Ward Allen came from a family of considerable wealth. But after he moved to Las Vegas and by the time Wendy met him, he was virtually penniless. Like so many, he had succumbed to whiskey, then lost his business, family, and money to the crushing need to get drunk.

Ward lost his life to drink, but he never lost his warmth. His alcoholic skin drooped like the skin of a boiled chicken, but nothing diminished Ward's smile. He was gentle, too, well-mannered and kind—he brought touches of humanity to the Ogden Avenue house. When Ward was around, everyone seemed happier. Tom would laugh. Amy giggled at the sweet cooing sounds he made to her. Even Gramby could smile.

Ward also was an able handyman. One day, Tom helped him with a rented backhoe as Ward positioned the massive machine and dug two deep holes out near his office. With the holes dug, Tom lowered down two sheet metal boxes, about a foot or more on each side. Wendy never saw what was inside the boxes, but imagined stolen jewelry, money, documents, IDs, or select possessions from some of Tom's victims. He also kept recordings of almost every phone call, all but those from Benny Binion. These included calls from Spilotro and mobsters from the Midwest and East Coast.

The box was covered with dirt and rocks and finally

capped with concrete that Ward had mixed, then smoothed with a trowel.

Ward made a little money from the work, happily spending it on drink. He did not, however, have a happy ending.

Two days later, Wendy was inside and Tom was behind the house feverishly tearing apart an air conditioner pump. There was a knock on the door. It was a Las Vegas cop, the one who usually stopped by to tip off Tom about any investigation involving him or the Binions.

"Ward Allen's dead," he told Wendy. They found the body in an outdoor hot tub, with a couple of empty bottles of vodka, not his usual drink, within reach. It looked like he'd had a stroke.

Wendy stumbled through the house to the back door, afraid to tell Tom, knowing he'd be devastated.

"Tom, Tom," she said. "It's Ward. Ward ..."

Tom stopped moving, his hands frozen inside the guts of the dead machine.

"What?" he said, looking up and smiling. "Ward is dead, isn't he?"

Wendy got light-headed and had to brace herself against the wall to keep from fainting. Tom pulled up a chair and sat her down, then walked to the front door and talked to the detective. He came back a few minutes later.

"Now, my little Winnerferd," he began. "Please don't cry and get yourself all upset over that drunk. He was stealing jewelry from me and selling it all over town. Ward was a big problem."

"But why Ward?" Wendy said through tears. "He was so kind to me. I liked Ward."

Tom pressed his case.

"Ward was no good," he said. "He never supported his

ex-wife and daughter who was born with cerebral palsy. He was nothing but a drunk."

Tom picked up the phone and called Ward's ex-wife, told her that he'd help set up Social Security payments for her and her daughter. He sounded so sincere, so caring, almost loving. And unmistakably pleased, Wendy thought, at being the one who was able to tell Ward's ex-wife about how she would benefit from her ex-husband's death.

❖ ❖ ❖

The body in the freezer. Ward Allen. Stories about Kennedy and Hoffa. Some real. Some, who knows? If they were meant to scare her into keeping silent, it worked.

Then there were times that the insanity of the Hanleys' life spilled into reality.

Four months pregnant in June 1976, Wendy and Tom drove eight blocks south to the Safeway supermarket at Charleston Boulevard and Maryland Parkway. Waiting to pay, a man standing behind Wendy made a playful comment about how good she looked.

That's all it took. Tom pulled a gun and pointed it at the man's head. Wendy ran outside to the truck. Stuffing the gun in his waistband, Tom followed.

He burned rubber on the hot May asphalt, but by the time he got to Gass Avenue a few blocks north, sirens and flashing lights were on his tail. He kept driving.

They got to their home. Squad cars were everywhere.

"Get out of my way, you son-of-bitches!" Tom yelled, as he pulled in front of the house. Cops crouched behind open car doors with pistols and shotguns pointed at Tom and Wendy.

The truck lurched to a stop, and Tom told Wendy to run into the house, lock the doors, and call their attorney.

Police pounded on the door, promising to break it in if she didn't open up. Police told reporters that Hanley got out of the truck, dropped his pistol, and kicked it under the truck. On the phone, the attorney told Wendy to open the door and let them in.

Police scoured the house, found some fifty rifles and pistols, took them all, and left. An hour later, Tom called from the sheriff's office. "They've got my guns," he said angrily, then to someone in the background, "I want my guns back!"

Then quieter on the phone: "I'll be home soon, in about an hour. Don't worry."

A few hours later, Wendy heard a car pull up and saw Tom get out of a squad car, wave to the officer driving, and walk into the house. He told her the sheriff had him sit in his office for a while to calm down. There'd be no charges. No arrest. And he'd get his guns back.

Police gave the local papers a different version of the incident. They said Hanley was arrested after pulling a gun in a dispute over too many items in the nine-item supermarket express line. Police also said Hanley had been jailed on three charges—reckless driving, failure to yield to police, and possession of a single stolen gun (the gun he used had been stolen during an April burglary). The papers also said he was jailed on $1,500 bail.

The charges were true. But Tom never went to jail. He never went to court. But for one terrified man with too big a mouth, it was as though it never happened.

The next day, Tom went to the sheriff's office and retrieved his guns.

❖❖❖

Sometimes, the stupid or the drunken get away with

things the sober and sane get killed for doing. In 1970, several years before Wendy came into the picture, Hanley was walking in front of the Four Queens on Fremont Street, when someone came up, hit him in the mouth, and walked on. Newspapers said the unknown assailant "escaped." They didn't add "with his life."

❖ ❖ ❖

Assault and battery, assault with a deadly weapon, burglary, resisting arrest, reckless driving, drug charges, kidnapping, and, finally, murder.

Over twenty-one years, Gramby Hanley had compiled a rap sheet totaling forty-five criminal charges. His arrest record with Las Vegas police from 1977 is topped with the warning: "Use Caution. Armed and Dangerous."

But he was more dangerous than any computer printout could portray.

By March 1975, three months after Tom buried his wife, Wendy moved into the house on Ogden. Her relationship with Gramby hadn't gone completely sour yet. That point was signaled in that year, however, when he gave Wendy a pencil-and-paper sketch. It was her, in perfect proportion, unsmiling.

"I like to sketch the faces of people I'm about to kill," he said.

Months later, Wendy said Gramby tried to kill her after she discovered some jewelry was missing. This was just after she sat with Tom and Gramby on their living room floor marveling at the heist the two men had just pulled at a jewelry store. Gold bracelets, watches, thin gold bars, gemmed rings, and diamond pins. It was a special moment, one she wouldn't forget. Not only did it afford her a moment of giggling, girlish laughter, but it was the moment Tom asked her to wed.

Wendy was trying on all the jewelry when Tom told her to pick out a favorite ring, the most expensive, best one she could find. She picked a huge diamond. He took it from her, held it up, and watched it glitter as he twisted it in the light, then slid it on her finger.

"Will you marry me?" he asked.

Without hesitation, without choice—because to wait or to say "maybe" could have meant the difference between living another day and dying that night—she said "yes" to the man nearly forty years her senior.

Gramby said nothing.

Making the bed late the next morning, she reached under the mattress to tuck in the sheets and didn't feel the satchel of jewelry she had stashed there. "Gramby!" she thought.

Tom was making breakfast.

"Tom, Gramby stole my jewelry! I'm going over to get it back."

She ran outside and around the corner to Gramby's house.

"Give it back, give it back!" she said, pounding on his door.

He opened the door.

"I'll call the police if you don't give my jewelry back!"

As the words left her lips, the blood left her extremities and she caught her heart in her throat. What was she saying? She backed away from the door, then ran as fast as she could toward her house. She wasn't fast enough. Gramby caught her, knocked her onto her back on the front lawn of her house and clamped his hands around her neck.

"I'm going to kill you! I'm going to kill you! Die, you little bitch!"

She couldn't move or breathe. Wendy thought she was going to die until she heard Tom's voice.

"Get off of her, Gramby! Get off of her now!"

He let go. Her vision was blurry but she saw Tom holding a gun to Gramby's head.

"Dad, the little bitch was going to rat!"

"I'll take care of this," Tom said coolly. "And don't you ever touch her again. Now get the hell out of here."

He helped Wendy up and put her in the pickup truck.

"How many times have I told you 'Silence is the fence around wisdom'?" he said angrily. "You know, even if you did go to the cops, word would get back to me before they showed up anywhere, including Gramby's place."

He started the truck. "I want to show you something," he said. He drove a bit, got about a block from Gramby's house, and stopped.

"See those guys with the suits standing on a chair behind that house?" he said.

There were three of them taking turns standing on a chair and looking over a fence using binoculars to get a closer look. They were looking into Gramby's backyard.

"Those are FBI agents," Tom said. "Been here for about a week off and on. Maybe that's why Gramby got so mad at you."

"He didn't have to try to kill me," Wendy protested. "You know I know better than to call the cops."

"And you know what would happen if you did, right?"

"Yeah, I do."

"Good girl," Tom said, grabbing her knee. "Now let's take a drive up to see Old Man Binion and have some lunch."

"Okay, Tom."

❖ ❖ ❖

Gramby did change. Once. For a very short time after he married, and he and his wife stopped doing heroin, cold turkey.

For two weeks, they locked themselves in one of the bedrooms in Tom's house. Wendy made stomach-soothing broth and washed their clothes as they suffered through the physical pain of drug withdrawal.

Then the miracle happened. After he'd gotten used to sunshine, to the feel of his own skin, to the weight of life, Gramby smiled. His personality changed. He was calm, less excitable.

Tom was tickled. He didn't care if Gramby's calm demeanor meant he'd leave the violence that Tom had raised him on. His greatest hope was for Gramby to leave drugs, exit society if he had to, find a cave or a cabin far from everyone and absorb himself in art.

In Tom's mind, drugs and nothing else had ruined his boy. He talked about it to Frank "Lefty" Rosenthal at Marie Callender's restaurant one day. Tom and Wendy met Rosenthal many times there to do business, at the place Rosenthal narrowly escaped death in the mid-1980s when he started his car and a bomb attached to the undercarriage detonated.

Rosenthal had a family drug problem of his own. His beautiful wife, Geri, was just as addicted to heroin as Gramby. In fact, Rosenthal blamed Gramby for supplying her with the drug.

There's a simple solution," Tom suggested. "Just get rid of her."

"I know," Rosenthal replied. "But she's the mother of my kids. Whaddya gonna do?"

One day a friend stopped by the house looking for Gramby. Gramby had sent Wendy outside to wait for the guy, who was going to deliver some drugs. He said he didn't want his dad to see whomever was showing up and asked Wendy to do him this one favor. Wendy wanted a better relationship with Gramby, so she said sure and stood outside by the curb.

Tom looked out the custom-tinted room windows and saw her. Then he saw the car drive up. He had just bought hundreds of dollars worth of art supplies for Gramby, hoping his son would absorb himself in his raw talent instead of drugs. The black man behind the wheel wasn't an art enthusiast.

Tom walked outside calmly, holding his pistol at his side, muzzle down. He walked to the driver's-side window and slammed the gun butt on the car's roof, denting it.

"Get the hell out of here!" he yelled. "Gramby doesn't want any of your drugs anymore!"

"Please don't kill me, Uncle Tom," the young man said. "We all know what you can do. Please don't kill me!"

"That's right," Tom said. "You know what happened to your dope-dealing buddies? I will burn you up the same way. Come around here again, and I'll shoot you in your dope-dealing head."

"Please, Mr. Tom, please, Uncle Tom, don't kill me. We know what you did to our brother, I don't want any trouble, Uncle Tom. Please, Mr. Tom, you won't see me ever around here again!"

"Then get the hell out of here."

"I will, I will," and the car sped away.

By that time, Gramby had sped out the back door, jumped the backyard fence and ran home.

Tom knew his dream for Gramby was nothing but that. A dream. Within a few months of quitting, Gramby was back on heroin again.

Even Tom's closest friends used drugs.

Al Bramlet, head of the powerful Culinary Union, a man who walked into a casino and received everything he wanted without even asking, snorted cocaine. It disgusted Tom, who would later wonder if all those drugs somehow changed Al, made it so he couldn't see the warning signs or so he could easily ignore the threats.

The reason's for Bramlet's murder may always be the center of debate, but his drug use undoubtedly made him an easier target for Tom to take out.

CHAPTER SIXTEEN

Al Bramlet's rise to power is the kind of bruising, fight-to-the-top story interchangeable with those of union leaders in the mid-1900s throughout the country.

In similar fashion, his demise came after a life of hubris and egotism, a sense of invincibility, and unheeded warnings.

One more similarity: The people who wanted Bramlet and other union heads out of the way may have hired the same killer: Tom Hanley.

❖ ❖ ❖

A few weeks after Bramlet's disappearance in February 1977, *Time* magazine summed up his notoriety in its March 14 issue:

"Even in Las Vegas, a town not noted for softies, Al Bramlet, fifty-nine, stood out as mean. The high-living, free-spending boss of Local 226 of the Culinary Workers Union … made enemies as effortlessly as gamblers throw dice."

Born in 1917, Bramlet was raised an Arkansas farm boy. The Navy drafted him during World War II. Las Vegas took him in 1946, about the same time that Tom Hanley moved to town. Having earned credibility as a business agent in a local bartenders union in Los Angeles after the war, Bramlet came to work with the Culinary Union. Membership in the union, chartered in 1938, totaled five hundred to one thousand members at the time.

By the mid-'50s, Bramlet had clawed his way to the top

of the heap, becoming the union's secretary-treasurer. He worked feverishly in the '50s to grow membership and find reliable employees. He traveled all across the country to recruit people who had never before considered moving to the brutal heat of the Mojave Desert for a job.

By the time of Bramlet's death, "his" union would number 27,000 members. Their dues not only enriched the union—while many thought Bramlet died a millionaire, his estate was estimated at around $300,000—they formed a powerful voting bloc. In a state with few registered voters, politicians ignored the Culinary at their own risk.

Bramlet was all-powerful in a city with an economic engine—the casinos—oiled and maintained by the labor of Bramlet's membership.

"When he walked into a casino, it was carte blanche," Barb, Bramlet's widow, told *Las Vegas Life* magazine. "He was treated like a king. He paid for nothing."

Bramlet's Culinary Union filled a dour building off Las Vegas Boulevard; a tough-looking place that satisfied members who thought it mirrored the union's persona. The reality, though, was that Bramlet spent a lot of his days and nights with the Las Vegas elite, chuckling and dining with the same casino execs his members expected him to fight against tooth and nail for benefits.

In a city where appearance means everything, it began to look like Bramlet was too friendly with the casinos. He didn't help himself, and probably didn't care what anyone thought anyway, by walking around with a little too much flash for someone who was supposed to be grubbing to make a living with the working man. Bramlet liked to wear gold jewelry, chain-smoked expensive cigarettes, wore brightly colored suits in the fashion of the day—the ubiquitous light-colored leisure suit with a broad-collared shirt beneath. The *L.A. Times* said he "had a reputation as a ladies man."

Wendy also knew of Bramlet's growing cocaine habit, because Tom often complained about his hatred for drugs spawned from Gramby's debilitating heroin addiction.

By the time of Bramlet's murder, his member bell captains had sued him. They claimed their leader had negotiated away their job of making arrangements for show tickets, rental cars, and other necessities for visitors. That meant the loss of up to $1,500 a month, a princely sum.

That was only part of the lawsuit, however. It also posed this question: If bell captains no longer had made arrangements for guests, guess who did? How about Bramlet? The suit alleged that Bramlet's name appeared as a principal in three businesses designed to take on those duties.

In a story after his disappearance, the *L.A. Times* quoted an unnamed source, speaking of Bramlet's penchant for collecting enemies: "There's no question he had enemies, just by the very nature of the work he does. And I'll bet you we have any number of guys in this town who would kill you just for practice."

Count among them the non-union business owners that Bramlet targeted for pickets and, when pickets didn't work, bombings. The Village Pub. The Starboard Tack. David's Place. The Alpine Village restaurant, one of the most popular places in Las Vegas, was both picketed, then bombed in late 1976.

In the small city, everyone seemed to believe that the Culinary—less known were the bombers themselves, Tom and Gramby—was behind the bombings, but police either had a hard time putting together a case or didn't want to. Still, the media put the questions to Bramlet.

When young television reporter Bob Stoldal told Bramlet about the rumors, the union boss tried to turn it around. Would it make sense, he countered, for the Culinary to bomb the very business it was trying to unionize?

"It's a rather funny coincidence that we have an election coming up at the Starboard Tack, and it seems odd to me that we'd have this bombing to try to discredit the union," he said. "It makes sense as far as discrediting this local union. And they're doing a fair good job of it."

Stoldal: "Will you cut back on pickets?"

"No, I will continue to picket."

Bramlet's disappearance presented investigators with the problem of narrowing the list of people who might like to see him dead. Restaurant owners? Casinos? His own union members? Or the mob, whose hands were still all over the casinos forced to hire union workers? What about drug dealers?

And, of course, Tom Hanley, who previously had been considered a person of interest in the murder of three other union leaders.

Hanley was one of Bramlet's best friends. Oasis Air Conditioning survived on just one customer, Bramlet's Culinary Union. In the few months before Bramlet's disappearance, Wendy and Tom walked him from his office to his car nightly.

But Hanley was a killer. Even if he'd never been convicted, police knew that. Maybe Bramlet forgot.

CHAPTER SEVENTEEN

"**A**l got stomped."

Tom hung up the phone. He stood looking at Wendy and sighed.

"Let's take a drive," he said. "We have to go meet Al."

It was the fall in 1976, a few months after the nation celebrated its two hundredth birthday, two hundred years of independence from British rule, two hundred years of growth in a country where society often boils down to the Golden Rule: Those with the gold make the rules.

In Las Vegas, Bramlet made the rules. His union's coffers, its pension fund, brimmed with $42 million. But others had more gold. More power. And absolutely no reservations about using deadly force if they needed to get someone out of the way. Or to get their hands on that pension fund.

That was the message Tony Spilotro and a couple of his torpedoes delivered to Bramlet in a downtown tavern. Various news reports speculate about the conflict that led to Bramlet's beating. Some say Spilotro wanted Bramlet to enroll union members in an insurance plan set up by Chicago mobsters.

They were desperate to do something. For decades a power in Las Vegas, the mob was losing its casino foothold as Wall Street took over and used stockholders, not mob money and influence, to fund growth.

This is how *Time* magazine summarized one theory behind Bramlet's disappearance:

"The reason, investigators say, may have been a quarrel Bramlet was having with the mob over the use—and presumably abuse—of a portion of the Culinary local's $42 million pension fund. Some $16 million of the fund has already been loaned out to resorts and developments that are backed by Las Vegas gambling bosses."

The magazine went on: "The latest proposal for dipping into the Culinary pot—reportedly cooked up by a Chicago Mafia triggerman named Tony Spilotro—called for founding a clinic-pharmacy where ailing union members would receive medical treatment and drugs. The mob would skim off funds for its own use.

"Bramlet had no objections, but he kept insisting on a bigger cut for himself. Says an investigator: 'He was demanding more out of the thing than the mob thought he should get.'"

Bramlet's resistance had consequences. That phone call to Tom and Wendy was just the beginning. But it scared him. Tom and Wendy saw that when they met Bramlet at the Culinary Union.

"Those punks from Chicago are trying to take over my union!" Bramlet spat. Blood dripped from cuts on his face. He trembled as Wendy cleaned his wounds. He stopped her for a moment, dipped a tiny spoon into a plastic bag of cocaine powder, and sniffed it in deep.

"I'll die before I hand my pension fund over to the International!" he said.

And why not fight? He'd built the fledgling union from nothing to a 27,000-member behemoth whose members could run a casino into the ground at the slightest wag of his finger. How dare anyone try to muscle in on what he'd created for his union, for the city of Las Vegas? For

twenty-four years he had been the union's shepherd, nur-
turing it and viciously fighting off anyone who tried to
hurt his flock.

That night the Teamsters had a meeting at the union hall.
Tom and Wendy walked Al to his car. Tom told Al he'd go
to the meeting. Joey Aiuppa from the Chicago Outfit would
be there. Tom promised to talk to him and straighten it out.

At the union hall, Tom went inside and came out a while
later. He got into the truck and shook his head.

"Joey Aiuppa wants me to knock some sense into Al,"
he said. "I told Al this was coming. He should have kept
a low profile, not throw around his power."

Tom ranted about a grocery list of mob allegations. That
Bramlet was stealing from the pension fund and sending
the money to an account in Switzerland, that he was prolonging strikes and protests by Culinary members.

"Al thinks no one can touch him." Tom understood that,
too. "He's my friend, Winnerferd. But I don't know if I'm
ready to take on my associates in Chicago and Kansas City."

Now Wendy was shaking. For as long as she knew Tom,
Bramlet was always right there—Tom's only customer, calling the air conditioning office every day, a part of their
ongoing conversation: "Al's going to Reno ... Aiuppa's got
a job for me to do."

For a man in a "business" that didn't allow close friend-
ships, Bramlet was as close to a friend as Tom had in
Las Vegas. The two arrived in town within years of each
other. Both became heavies in their respective unions. Each
lived through violent struggles for worker rights. They
understood each other. They struggled with the same issues—gangsters, casinos, members, and a personal life
on the side.

Tom grimaced as he drove home. "Al is a dead man if he doesn't go International with the union."

"Tom, can't you do something to help him?" Wendy pleaded.

"I can't now," Tom replied. "It's gone too far."

For the next three months until Bramlet's disappearance, Tom and Wendy drove over to Bramlet's office at day's end.

CHAPTER EIGHTEEN

After that night, phone calls to the Ogden Avenue house from Chicago, and from Benny Binion, Harry Claiborne, and Ben Schmoutey, Bramlet's right hand for two decades, became more frequent. Wendy had no idea what they talked about. She'd answer the phone and give it to Tom. Tom normally told her everything. Not this time. Gramby, too, started coming over more often and having quiet talks with Tom in the back room.

Wendy was concerned but not as much as before. Amy was born in November 1976 and she focused her soul on her little girl. Amy was the perfect antidote to the Machiavellian plans and deadly outcomes to come.

Tom doted on Amy, too, and like any parent—or perhaps more so—he was equal to the task of killing anyone who came close to threatening his offspring. Even if that meant the possibility of killing another one of his kids.

A few weeks after Amy's birth, the four of them—Tom, Gramby, Wendy, and Amy—had Thanksgiving dinner at Wendy's mom's house. She put Amy to sleep in another room as the adults sat and talked.

Suddenly Tom sat upright in his chair.

"Where's Gramby?" Tom asked.

Wendy looked around. "He must be with Amy."

"What?!" Tom said, dashing into the bedroom.

Tom and Wendy saw Gramby leaning over with his

hands inside the bassinette, hidden but close to the baby's face, as if he were cradling little Amy Colleen's chin.

Tom grabbed Gramby's hands and pulled them up. He was holding a baby pillow.

"What the hell are you doing?" Tom demanded.

Gramby barely stirred. "Just playing with the little rugrat."

"She's asleep, goddammit," Tom said. "Get out of here."

Wendy's heart was caught in her throat.

"What? Did you think I was up to something?" Gramby asked with a smirk.

Gramby held up his hands in a "Hey, no problem, everything's cool" gesture. He dragged his feet as he walked out, smiling at Wendy.

"What was that all about? What was he doing?" Wendy asked.

"I don't want that high son of a bitch near our baby," Tom said. "He stays the hell away from her."

It terrified Wendy that the man she only knew as fearless worried about Gramby around her baby.

"I don't want him near Amy," she said.

"I need him now," Tom insisted. His voice was softer and assuring now. "We're working on something big. Don't worry about it. I've got it all worked out."

CHAPTER NINETEEN

Gramby came to the house early on February 24th wearing a tailored, black, pinstriped suit and fedora.

"Get rid of the hat," Tom said, shaking his head.

"Winnerferd, could you go in the closet and pick out a nice suit for me to wear, too?" he asked.

Tom was dressing in the bedroom when the phone rang. Wendy answered. It was Ed Hanley of the International union for Tom. Tom grabbed the receiver and listened for a second. "It'll be taken care of today," he replied, then told Hanley to "expect a call from the Dunes later today."

As Tom and his son walked out the door, Wendy asked what was going on.

"We just have to take care of something," Tom said. He was carrying extra clothes under his arm. He told Wendy to keep track of everyone who called the house. "We have a big meeting with the boys from Chicago."

Tom knew all of Bramlet's moves, having spent so much time as his recent bodyguard and his longtime union enforcer. He knew that on that morning, Bramlet had flown to Reno for union decertification hearings at Harolds Club. Bramlet's flight was due back a little after four p.m.

He intended to meet Bramlet at the airport—but not to give him a friendly ride home. He had plans, beginning with getting drunk with his employee, Eugene Vaughn, who had called earlier that day. Vaughn, a sheet metal worker, had worked fifteen years for Tom. He called because he was owed fifteen hundred dollars. Tom didn't have the money, but he told Vaughn that Bramlet did. So the two got drunk, agreeing to meet Al after he touched down at McCarran.

Later, in court, Vaughn said he drove Tom to the air conditioning shop where Tom picked up something. Then they drove to the airport and parked next to Bramlet's gray, 1973 Lincoln Continental in Section K, Space No. 5.

Gramby showed up in his Cutlass a bit later. Tom got out and walked into the airport with his son to check on the Reno flight.

"Stay here," Tom instructed Vaughn after walking back outside. "We'll be right back."

He and Gramby drove away and returned a bit later with a rented light blue van. All three got inside and waited. For insurance, so that Bramlet wouldn't get away, Tom told Vaughn to let some air out of the tires of Bramlet's car.

About 4:30 p.m., Bramlet had deplaned and called the Culinary Union office from an airport phone. His daughter was there and took the phone from the receptionist.

"Go on home," he told her. "I'll be right there."

But as he walked to his car, he was met by Tom and Vaughn.

"I need that money," Tom said.

"You'll get what you're owed," Bramlet said.

Suddenly, Gramby sprang from the van and stuck a gun in Bramlet's back. "I'll kill you right here if you don't get into the van."

"You get in, too," Tom ordered Vaughn.

In the van, Gramby handcuffed Bramlet, then tied his hands and ripped a piece of duct tape from a roll and stuck it over Bramlet's mouth. Bramlet laid face down on the floor. Tom drove; Vaughn sat in the passenger seat.

No one talked.

Tom was driving west on Blue Diamond Road when he suddenly jerked the wheel and turned south onto a desert road. They stopped after a few minutes and everyone got out. Gramby undid the rope and handcuffs and tore off the tape.

"Don't get excited, Al," Tom said. "Nobody's going to hurt you."

He kept the ruse going, letting Bramlet take a welcome swig from a pint of whiskey. His hopes soared. Maybe they weren't going to do anything. Maybe they just wanted to scare him. If this was really about the money, then he'd taken care of it with that phone call, hadn't he? Besides, he and Tom had known each other for so long. They were different but cut from the same cloth. He'd go as far as to call Tom a friend. Sure, Tom was a bit crazy. You had to be to do what he did for money. But he wouldn't kill a friend, would he?

Maybe Bramlet was too scared to remember the names of Alphonse Bass and James Hartley. And Ralph Alsup, who was also killed on the same night he had returned from a union meeting back in 1966.

They only stopped for a minute, anyway, before Tom, Gramby, and Bramlet got back into the van and talked about fifteen minutes.

Minutes later they were at the crest of the mountain farther just outside the Mountain Springs Saloon. From an outdoor pay phone, they called Syd Wyman, a well-known poker player and an executive at the Dunes. Gramby and

Vaughn helped Bramlet to the phone, his legs shaking so badly he couldn't hold himself up.

Bramlet told Wyman what he was ordered to tell him: Grab ten thousand dollars and deliver it to the Horseshoe "as a personal loan" to be paid back later.

On the other end of the line, Wyman was mystified. He quickly phoned Benny Binion, who claimed he was just as puzzled.

After the call, they drove back toward Las Vegas from the 5,400-foot crest of the mountain, then pulled off onto another dirt road, maybe the same one they had stopped on before. The drive took a while, with the hard-packed road dipping and twisting, rising and falling over steep inclines and deep gullies.

For a brief moment, through an opening in the foothills, Bramlet would have caught the faintest light emanating from the Las Vegas Strip. It would have been his last view of his beloved city. If they'd kept driving, they eventually would have run into Goodsprings, a tiny town spawned from a mining boom sixty years earlier, and home to the fifty-year-old Pioneer Saloon, which proudly maintained a bullet hole in the wall, the shooting of which is said to have killed a man who still haunts the barroom.

Finally, they stopped and everyone got out. Vaughn saw Tom grab the silenced .22 from Gramby.

"Hey, Al," he said. As Bramlet turned, Tom shot him in the head.

"The gun went 'pap,'" Vaughn testified.

Tom stood over the body and unloaded four or five more shots into it. Gramby dragged Bramlet's body down the hill out of sight. Then he came up alone and told them to come down there.

Gramby had stripped the body naked. Even in the pitch black, what little light shone from the sliver of moon that night made his body glow. The three stared at it, mesmerized. Tom broke that reverie by firing four or five more slugs into the body, just to make sure it was a corpse. Then he told Vaughn to help bury it.

Gramby poured white lime powder on the body before covering it with rocks. Walking away, Vaughn looked back to see uncovered patches of skin shining between spaces in the rocks.

From court testimony, Gramby was said to have tossed Bramlet's bloody clothes out the window. That didn't happen, according to Wendy. Tom kept the clothes and later, as law enforcement closed in, he had Gramby bury them in the middle of the night.

Tom dropped off Gramby and Eugene at the airport. Gramby got a cab, Vaughn drove his own car, dazed and terrified back to his home in Henderson.

❖ ❖ ❖

Tom and Gramby drove slowly up to the Ogden Avenue house. Tom wasn't wearing a suit anymore. He had on the clothes that he had carried with him. He smiled wanly at Wendy. She'd never seen him like this before. He appeared dazed as he walked to the fireplace and stared at the burning logs. She stood next to him.

"You know I love my Winnerferd very much," he said quietly and held her tight.

He smelled different. If she'd known what he had just done, she would have said he smelled like blood. Her mind searched wildly for a clue as to what had happened, what he'd been doing.

"I'm going to clean up," he said, and as he moved away Wendy noticed dark spots covering his hands and jacket.

Tom stripped off his clothes and threw them into the washing machine. He yelled, "Wendy, can you bring me some clean pants?"

He was emptying his jacket pockets when she walked in with his pants.

"Look at this," he said, excitement in his voice. He held up a tiny object between his thumb and index finger. "It's a rare tiger-eye ring."

"Ooh, that's pretty," Wendy said. "Where did you get it?"

"Well, don't you recognize it?"

"No—should I?"

Tom's blue eyes shifted from her to the doorway. Gramby stood there watching.

"Wendy, we have some business to talk about," Tom said.

Wendy hurried into the other room, stopping when the door closed behind her.

"Where's the key?" she heard Tom ask.

"I gave you everything that was there, Dad," Gramby shot back.

"Look," Tom said, his voice low and gruff. "You *better* find that key or we are going to have problems."

Wendy went into little Amy's room, picked up her baby, and held her tight as she tilted forward and back in the rocking chair. Something was wrong. Different. She'd never seen that before, the stressed whispers, the—was it fear she heard in Tom's voice? Then the way he hugged her and professed his love. The brown spots on his clothes. And where did that ring come from?

The ring scared her most of all. Whoever it belonged to was at the center of whatever those two had done. And she was sure they had done something very bad. She wanted to bolt. To pick up Amy and a blanket and just run.

Then what?

No. Everything would be fine. Tom did crazy things. Sure, he killed people. But she convinced herself that he had a baby now, a child he loved with his heart. He wouldn't jeopardize his daughter's future. He had probably given up the killing and bombing. He wouldn't do that, knowing that if he ever got caught, he'd lose his little Goosier.

Tom poked his head into the baby's room. "Well, I'm going to bed."

"I'll join you as soon as Amy falls asleep."

She laid Amy in the bassinette, then pulled the small walled bed into their bedroom. That night, she didn't want her little girl to sleep alone.

CHAPTER TWENTY

The next day was a Friday and cool again in the sixties. Tom woke up earlier than usual and during breakfast said he wanted to go for a ride out to their five acres near Pahrump. Benny Binion had given it to them as a wedding gift. Tom said he wanted to plant three trees—one each for Mom, Dad, and Amy.

Blue Diamond Road leads directly west from Las Vegas over a five thousand-foot mountain, then down into the Pahrump Valley. On the way, Tom suddenly pulled off and started driving south on the desert road they usually took to go shooting on Sundays.

"Oh, are we going to shoot?" Wendy asked.

"No, I just want to take a look."

After a few minutes he stopped, got out of the truck, and turned himself around as he scanned the sagebrush, the Joshua trees, and tan and white rock for as far as the eye could see.

Satisfied, he jumped back in the truck, did a Y-turn, and pulled back onto Blue Diamond Road. When they got to Pahrump half an hour later, they stopped at a nursery and bought three trees. They drove back toward Las Vegas and stopped at their five-acre plot. Tom dug three holes, planted one tree. Then he threw a sock into the second hole, put the tree in over it, and covered it with dirt.

"Remember which tree that sock is under," he said.

"Why, what's in it?"

"Just some jewelry."

Old Man Binion's ranch was out that way, too. Tom stopped and said he had to run inside for a second. For the first time since she'd known him, he didn't invite her in to meet Binion together. Some thirty minutes later he came back out with some fresh honey and they drove home.

That was the last quiet moment the three would have together before Tom died. The phone was ringing when they got home. It was Barb Bramlet, Al's wife. She sounded scared. She knew what Tom was capable of doing. "Something's happened to Al," she said. "I need to talk to Tom."

Tom was out back, talking quietly to himself and whomever else, gutting the innards of an old air conditioner.

"Tom, Barbara Bramlet's on the phone and she's crying."

He said nothing but walked straight into the house and got on the phone.

"Do you want me to come over?" he said after a few minutes of trying to calm her down. "Maybe he just decided to stay another night in Reno."

After he hung up, he sighed.

"Something has happened to Al. I don't know what. But I'm going to find out. Whatever you do, don't let anyone in the house, and don't answer the phone."

But the phone rang just then. It was Schmoutey, Bramlet's second-in-command.

Then he was back outside and into the pickup with Wendy and Amy. "Al's missing, and I have to talk to Schmoutey," he said. They drove to the Culinary Union office. "Wait right here," he said, looking Wendy in the eyes.

He went inside. Wendy held onto Amy, her mind reeling. That ring. Then her body started to tremble, and her stomach shook little Amy as she began to cry. The ring looked just like the one Al wore on his pinky. Or was it? Was she just putting two and two together because Al was missing and they were here at the union office and Barb Bramlet had just called?

Tom hurried out the front door, got into the truck, and threw a four-inch bundle of cash on the car seat. He drove away steadily and they stopped at a supermarket. Wendy went inside to buy something to make for dinner while Tom took a roll of quarters and his brown, tattered diary full of phone numbers and marched to the pay phone.

She came out fifteen minutes later, and he stayed on the phone for another ten.

On the short drive home, Wendy had to ask. "Tom, whose ring was that you showed me last night?"

His jaw muscles bulged as he clenched his teeth. He turned to Wendy, his eyes looking bluer and colder than she remembered.

"Remember, Wendy, silence is the fence around wisdom."

Fear, anger, worry, sadness—Wendy buried it all in an instant, knowing that if she asked too much or showed anything again, she'd be dead.

"Tom, you can trust me."

❖ ❖ ❖

Barbara Bramlet hadn't just called Tom. Before seven o'clock that morning, she also called Michael Pisanello, an assistant at the Culinary Union. Pisanello drove around to Bramlet's usual haunts to see if he could be found. He wasn't at the Dunes. Or at the apartment he kept at the Jockey Club. His car was still parked at the airport.

The police were called, and, from the criminal complaint, learned only a few facts that day. First, they checked the airport and found Bramlet's car, which was photographed. Later that day investigators talked to Bramlet's wife. They also talked to Wyman at the Dunes, having him retell the strange story about the $10,000 personal loan to be sent to Binion's Horseshoe.

Two days later, police interviewed Rebecca Sanford, a stewardess for Hughes Air West. Sanford remembered Bramlet on the flight back from Reno, having recognized him from numerous flights before. Detectives also checked the airline manifest for Flight No. 35 back to Las Vegas and confirmed that Bramlet was on board.

They also talked to Ben Schmoutey, heir to the Culinary if Bramlet was out of the way. Schmoutey said Bramlet had been in Reno for decertification hearings. Then he added some information about Tom Hanley: that a check had been written out to Hanley but was held, at Bramlet's request, because Hanley hadn't completed a job at the Culinary Union.

As those two detectives worked the edges, Tom acted like everything was normal back home. He talked so much about Al wanting to steal pension fund money that Wendy began to believe he had actually skipped town, perhaps fleeing to Switzerland where Tom said he held a bank account unlockable only with a key Bramlet wore around his neck.

She began to relax again.

"Let's go out to Henderson and see Gene," Tom said.

It was February 26th, and the drive to Henderson to Vaughn's house was welcome because Wendy knew Gene's daughter-in-law and liked to see some of the old landmarks in the area where she had ridden her horse, Red, just a few years earlier.

At Vaughn's house, Tom and Gene talked by his truck. Gene's daughter-in-law took Wendy into the house.

"Wendy, do you know what's going on?" she asked, looking to the front door to see if anyone could hear.

"No, what?"

Right then Tom burst in, his face reddened with anger, and started yelling.

"Your father-in-law is a drunk, and if you or your husband says anything about his drunken talk, I will bring all of you down! Do you understand?" He towered over Gene's daughter-in-law.

"Let's go, Wendy."

Tom sprayed dust into the air as he U-turned the pickup and gunned it back toward town.

"That Gene Vaughn," he muttered to himself. "He needs to be taken care of."

CHAPTER TWENTY-ONE

It was a perfect storm for the media: the disappearance of a powerful union man from a city all but spawned from union money lent to mobsters to build a gambling empire.

Even if it took three days for the papers to catch on.

The day before Bramlet's disappearance, the *Las Vegas Sun*'s top story told of Governor Mike O'Callaghan signing an order for Strip casinos to turn off their signs during the day to conserve energy. The next day, Thursday, February 24th, two front-page stories detailed a new equal rights amendment push and fears that gasoline prices, about sixty cents a gallon, might rise five cents by September.

When Barbara Bramlet began calling the police and the union frantically Friday morning, the *Sun*'s front-page story was about a Rancho High School girl suing to try out for the boys' baseball team. The next day included some garden-variety union/mob stuff: "Feds take Teamsters to trial on pensions" and "Frontier Hotel dealers charge union busting" next to a photo of a space shuttle piggybacking on a 747 for a test flight in California.

Bramlet's story finally hit the papers on Sunday, February 27th. "Cops baffled by Bramlet disappearance/Search intensifies." A smaller story on the front page told of two Las Vegas twentysomethings being charged with killing their roommate. Someone stumbled upon the roommate's body near Mountain Springs, a popular place to dispose of the dead. Bramlet's moldering body wasn't much farther

away, but it wouldn't be discovered for at least another
two weeks.

Now Bramlet's disappearance led the newspapers for
weeks. "Union posts reward," then "Dunes' Sid Wyman
asked $10,000 for Al Bramlet," and "FBI takes active roll in
Bramlet search." The story about Wyman and the $10,000
included a transcribed conversation between a *Sun* reporter and Benny Binion, who played dumb. Asked if
he knew why Bramlet had asked for the $10,000, Binion
replied: "No. Frankly, I couldn't understand the whole
conversation. I was half drunk, so when I hung up I went
to sleep and forgot all about it."

The $10,000 figure would become crucial toward coming
up with a motive, true or not, for the killing. The Hanleys
would later say Bramlet owed them $10,000, money not
paid for the bombings they rigged on the Culinary Union's
behalf.

Bob Stoldal, reporter for the local CBS affiliate, Channel
8, saved his typewritten notes and practice scripts from
those days. Yellowed almost forty years later, they read as
dispatches of urgency as he works out what he'll say on
camera, then adds mid-thought a reminder to buy someone
a drink to get more information.

"May have been a suspect in the attempted fire bombings at two local restaurants about a month ago. -0- got
to push ... mal ... see if he, see if he will be deep throat
... just confirmation ... call mal for a drink ..." Another
note: "GAVE HIM WISKEY(sic) ... Check see if russel can
get any information."

CHAPTER TWENTY-TWO

On March 17, 1977, St. Patrick's Day, Barbara Norman and her husband drove deep into the desert on a dirt road off of Blue Diamond Road. Stopping to take a walk, Barbara went one way, her husband the other. Wearing sandals, her feet began to hurt, so she walked to the bottom of a gully to find more level ground. That's when she saw it.

The long oval shape of the sharp desert rocks piled higher on one end than the other struck her at once as a grave. She ran and found her husband, who first pooh-poohed the notion. He walked up to the rocks and kicked a few from the top, then backed away.

Long and white, Al Bramlet's fingers rested on his stomach, jutting from a pair of cold steel handcuffs.

❖ ❖ ❖

While a Channel 8 news crew filmed, police and the district attorney stood around the body awaiting crime scene analysts. Police didn't have to put up "Do Not Cross" tape. In the Las Vegas of the 1970s, police and news people drank together. They knew the rules.

The vintage video unfolds:

Lieutenant Beecher Avants, sideburns creeping hippie-ishly close to his jaw line, walks up to the camera, and a reporter starts asking questions.

"We got a call to come down and meet these two people, a man and his wife at the Mountain Springs bar up here, and they were quite excited naturally," Avants says. "They thought they had found a body. It seems like the person we had been looking for."

In the background someone chuckles, and the news microphone picks up a whisper from District Attorney George Holt: "No smiling. It's disrespectful."

Later, someone is pounding a wooden stake into the ground. "Driving a stake through his heart?"

"Yeah."

Later, two people lifted Bramlet in a body bag and carried him away.

❖ ❖ ❖

Chuck Lee, the homicide detective, had to laugh. But for a portion of his body eaten away by wild animals, Bramlet looked like he'd been shot yesterday.

Police found Bramlet's body covered with lime. They guessed that this was a mistake, because lime acts as a preservative without moisture. So they found Bramlet with little decay. In fact, Tom told Wendy they intended to preserve the body because they wanted to move it to Reno to make it look like he was killed there.

❖ ❖ ❖

Vaughn had spilled the entire story to police more than a week before the body was found. Of course, when police heard Vaughn's story, so did Benny Binion, who called the house on Ogden Avenue.

Wendy gave the phone to Tom, who listened all of ten seconds.

"Okay, I'm out of here," he said and hung up.

Minutes later, Gramby showed up. Tom's sister, Jane, drove them to the home of one of Wendy's sisters in Henderson. Tom used the phone to make several calls to

Los Angeles. He didn't tell Wendy what was going on, but said he and Gramby had to get to Los Angeles.

"You've got to stay here with the baby until we get things straightened out," he said. Wendy nodded.

He had more instructions. She had to pick up money from Benny Binion at the Horseshoe, then get back to her sister's house and wait for his call.

"Is everything going to be okay, Tom?"

He looked at her with a beatific smile. "Do you think I'd let anything happen to your old Tom?"

Wendy drove to the Horseshoe. Benny walked behind the cashier's cage, picked up a bundle of bills totaling $10,000, and gave it to her. Then he told her what was coming next.

"There are going to be homicide cops over at your house later," he said. At seventy-two, Binion still had a sharp mind and spoke with authority and clarity. He was in fixer mode, laying down instructions as if he were reading them from a card. "Answer the door. Be nice to them. But under no circumstances do you give them any information on the whereabouts of Tom and Gramby."

"Okay, Mr. Binion. I'll be cool and calm."

"Good!" he said with a cheerful lilt. "We knew we could count on our stringy-haired little girl."

❖ ❖ ❖

At home, Wendy tried sitting but ended up standing in the middle of the living room. Waiting. Wondering. And terrified. Self-preservation taught her to hold back any sign of distress around Tom. But these were cops. Evil by Tom's code, but by hers? She didn't like cops. She associated them with some of the worst moments of her life—taking her brother Michael away, taking them all to foster homes,

sneering at her at the hospital after she had cut her wrists.
But did she even like Tom, let alone love him? Was Tom
the best alternative?

She pushed the thought out of her head. But what if they
walked in and she simply melted? Told them everything?
She had no idea what she'd do, and had no idea which
route was the safest.

Around six p.m., three hard raps rattled the front door.
Amy was in a back room with Gramby's ex-wife, Pat. Wendy
invited three homicide detectives inside and asked them
to sit. Chuck Lee and another detective remained standing.
The third, Lieutenant Beecher Avants, sat down like he
owned the place, legs spread and arms stretched to make
sure he used up every inch of the armrest and completely
filled the easy chair. She saw a man in his element and
felt the hairs stand on the back of her neck.

Avants couldn't care less what she thought. She wasn't
his main concern. For years he'd been after the Hanleys.
He knew they were bombing and killing, some of it at
the behest of Bramlet and the Culinary Union. Some of
the crimes ordered by Las Vegas' own version of the mob.
Some of them from Chicago.

"This shit is going to stop right now," he thought. "We're
going to drive this shit right into the ground."

Having overseen Metro's homicide and robbery details
for eight years and been commended numerous times,
Avants was police royalty. You don't get the plum homicide
job without a stellar record and some major cases under
your belt. He had led the 1974 probe into the sensational
murder of Hilda Krause, the seventy-one-year-old wife of
a Caesars Palace slots manager. In 1971 he directed the
investigation that led to the arrest of Barnell Bishop, who

robbed a dry cleaning business, then burned the owners to death.

Bramlet was bigger than both of those put together. Avants relished the challenge.

"We'd like to talk to Tom," Avants' voice boomed, making the room, the house, even more of his own.

"He had to go to a union meeting," she lied. He wouldn't be home for days.

"Well, we need to talk to Tom about Al Bramlet. You see, Mr. Bramlet seems to have disappeared," Avants said. He looked like he was having fun, even as he peered up through the massive panes of optical glass held to his face by wire frames.

If Wendy had felt fear before, Avants' coarse threat washed it away quickly. Now she was pissed.

"Tom has nothing to do with Al Bramlet's disappearance," she said with defiance. "He's the father of my baby. What gives you the right to say he has anything to do with Al Bramlet?"

Avants knew Las Vegas from the underbelly. Reveled in it. Knew what people under pressure would say before they even spoke. That was freedom to him. The hunt gave him even more freedom—to do or say almost anything he pleased. He loved Wendy's indignity because he expected it.

"Why?" he asked with no understated condescension. "Tom is the first person I always look for first when someone disappears. He's been questioned on several disappearances and murders over the years."

Wendy wanted to wipe the smug off his face.

"Al Bramlet is Tom's best friend! Tom is very, very concerned about where he might be."

Avants acted like he hadn't heard a word, as though this

was still his house. He stood up and walked toward Wendy. He was taller than Tom. He felt her shrink. She looked at the floor but he knew he'd put out the fire in her eyes. It would only be a matter of time.

"I hear you and Tom have a new baby," he said, his voice quieter now. "If you don't want anything to happen to that child, you better tell us everything you know about where Al Bramlet is."

Pat walked in from the back room holding Amy. If police wanted to talk any more to Wendy, she said, they'd have to wait for an attorney.

Avants put his hands on his hips and beamed a "well, what have we got here, little lady?" smile. He'd just been double-teamed, but if he felt stymied, he didn't look it. He seemed to genuinely appreciate the challenge.

"Fine, fine," he said. "Wendy, you have my card. Remember what I said."

Wendy began to shake and sob. The dozen cops who surrounded their pickup truck after the supermarket incident held none of the gravity, filled her with none of the dread she felt as the detectives walked to their car.

CHAPTER TWENTY-THREE

Tom called Wendy at her sister's house at 10:30 the next morning.

His instructions were brief: Go to the Horseshoe. Get the keys to Gramby's Olds Cutlass and another $10,000 from Teddy Binion. Leave Amy with her mom and drive to Los Angeles. When she got there, call this number and ask for "Blackie."

"I don't want to leave my baby with anyone!" she resisted.

"Please, Winnerferd, just do as I say. Those sons-a-bitches are trying to railroad me again for something I didn't do!"

He was so emphatic, his voice so strong with emotion, that she believed him. Something else must have happened, or someone else did it. He really *wouldn't* kill Al, just like she told the detectives. They were friends, and he was a new dad who loved his baby.

"Okay, Tom, let me get Amy settled and I'll get going."

"That's my little Winnerferd." She could hear his smile over the phone. "Oh, and bring me a couple guns, too!"

At the Horseshoe, Teddy looked worried as he handed over the keys and the cash, then grabbed her hand. "I don't know what's going on, but watch out for you and you alone."

"You know me, Teddy, I can take care of myself."

"I know you can, you're a pretty strong girl."

With two guns, $10,000, and Gramby's Cutlass, she arrived in Los Angeles about five hours later. Tom and a man named Pinky drove up in Pinky's movie-perfect pink Cadillac. Sporting a black pinstriped suit, ruby-in-gold pinky ring, and a big cigar, Pinky was a mobster straight out of Central Casting, except for his large-frame, gold-rimmed Elvis glasses. Pinky drove both of them to meet Blackie at a restaurant.

Then Tom and Wendy drove hours north to San Jose, where they met a bedraggled Gramby, his eyes bloodshot and his skin ashen from heroin withdrawal.

Tom announced that he would be selling the house and they would move to Phoenix. Las Vegas wasn't the city it used to be, he said. Al was gone. He'd need a new place to find work. It was said with such pragmatic, matter-of-fact simplicity that if you'd heard only the words without knowing who said them, it would have sounded perfectly reasonable. He hugged Wendy after the announcement, smiling at this new direction for himself, his wife, and baby.

In San Jose, attorney Harry Claiborne called and told him Bramlet's body had been found. Tom's reply chilled Wendy: "Well, what are they making such a big thing out of him anyway? He was just a little peon."

Wendy flew back to Las Vegas and her mom met her at the airport. "Let me take care of the baby until things get back to normal," she pleaded.

Wendy stifled a laugh. If Mom only knew what "normal" meant in the Hanley house. She couldn't tell her. She wouldn't believe it, or she'd never let Wendy go back. "Okay, Mom, but just for a few days."

"Good girl. You'll see. Everything is going to be all right."

Exhausted but unable to sleep, Wendy got right to packing. Tom's suits. Baby pictures. She found a box for all the handguns and rifles. She also noticed the freezer in the back of the house. It was no longer padlocked. It was open, empty, and bleached clean. "Old Joe" was gone.

Two days later, after she'd gotten much of their stuff into storage, police returned with a search warrant and combed the house, picking up hairs, notes, clothes. Unsmiling, burly rank-and-file cops took the guns and rummaged through her packed boxes before leaving.

Wendy walked over to the washing machine. Just to check. Tom's clothes from that night were still there, the sleeves of the jacket stained with tiny brown stains, which she now knew had to be blood. Al Bramlet's blood.

❖ ❖ ❖

The next day, Tom's attorney, Charlie Gardner, picked up Wendy and the two flew to Phoenix. After talking for several hours with Huey and Gramby, Tom emerged from a room and sat across from Wendy. There'd be no going back to Las Vegas, he said. Amy would be safe with her mom and sister. He had plans but they'd get messed up if he had to worry about Wendy getting snatched back in Las Vegas.

Wendy just cried.

Over the next three to four weeks, Tom and Wendy moved constantly, driving to Los Angeles and San Jose, then back to Phoenix. Tom was in constant motion. At every stop, he called Old Man Binion or Claiborne to catch the news from Las Vegas.

Back in Phoenix, Tom gave Wendy another assignment: Drive back to Las Vegas in the middle of the night and get another $10,000, this time from Teddy. She also was to pick up Debbie, who would be driving back to Phoenix with Wendy to deliver a silencer to Tom.

They sped down the highway, and as they crept over

Hoover Dam, Wendy asked where Debbie kept the silencer. If police stopped them and found it, they'd both go to jail.

"Don't worry, I've got it in a safe place," Debbie winked. She whelped as they hit a bump. She squealed when Wendy ran over a large divot in the road.

"What's the matter with you?"

"Remember I told you I had the silencer in a safe place," Debbie smiled weakly. "It's up my pussy and, boy, is this a bumpy trip!"

Wendy pulled over as tears streamed down her face from laughing so hard. It felt good, like she hadn't laughed in years.

CHAPTER TWENTY-FOUR

The Phoenix home was small estate, built not to fit into its hot, dry climate, but to create the suburban dream of the typical Midwest middle class. A golf-course green lawn, apple trees in the backyard, and elms out front.

Builders didn't bother to lay insulation in the attic or the walls. Who needed insulation when the temperature rarely dipped below fifty? That's shorts-and-T-shirt weather back in Illinois. Braced to the roof with thick metal bands, two massive central air-conditioning units blew twenty-four hours a day.

Tom wore a sweater but the cool air kept him alert. That was good because he still hadn't come to the end of his mental chess match, the climax of which would employ murder, extortion, and bribery. If all failed, he also had a last resort: Make a deal.

Now sixty years old, an arrest and conviction probably meant Tom would die in prison. But what about Gramby? Tom still saw good in that kid, his son. The thought of Gramby rotting in prison turned Tom's stomach in a way the killing of Al Bramlet or any of the others never did.

Sure, Gramby would do time. Tom knew that much, but he also knew Gramby might earn a get-out-of-prison-early deal if he and Tom became snitches. Not simply by dishing on the murders and the men who hired him because of his well-honed ability to kill efficiently, without malice or screw-ups. They'd drool over a deal like that. But they'd play hardball, too. They wouldn't just roll over because he gave them the Outfit and the corrupt unions. He had to create complications for the investigation. If he could hide or destroy enough evidence, the gun, the jewelry cleaned from Al's corpse. His attorney would brand Vaughn a delusional drunk. Maybe Vaughn really fired the shots. Maybe Vaughn even disappeared.

Moves had to be made quickly, though, because his attorney, Charlie Garner, was already arranging Tom and Gramby's surrender to the FBI and Las Vegas authorities.

He had to finish a few things. Tonight.

A corner of his lip curled up at the little trouper Wendy had turned out to be. All along he'd been right—to trust her, to marry her, to have a child with her.

But there was no other way. He had to do it.

His stomach churned and he rubbed his jaw, massaged his temples. The looseness of the skin on his face stunned him. Time's running out. He'd had a long, good life. He'd married, raised children. He'd do anything for those kids, every one of them. As for those who died at his hands, he couldn't muster sympathy or anything close to guilt. None of them was without fault. For that matter, no one on the planet was without fault. Everyone, in some way could deserve to die. Even him.

Even Wendy.

He'd go with her to Nevada tonight. It'd be her last trip. His, too, at least as a free man.

❖ ❖ ❖

Tom looked old. Circles under his eyes were dark as bruises. He winced and put a hand to his lower back as he rose from a chair. His aura wasn't so dark, even a little pinkish. It was a good reminder to Wendy. No one was either all good or all bad. We're all shades of both. Wendy didn't need to see auras to know that. Even in her hitman husband, she saw it in the gentle way he held Amy. In his hopes for Gramby. Even when he pulled a gun in defense of her honor, he demonstrated his capacity to love.

He hugged her firm but not too hard.

"They're moving in on us, Wendy." He was hoarse. "Me and Gramby are going to be arrested for the murder of Al Bramlet."

He outlined his next moves. Murder. Bribes. And using Robert Peoples, a recently released felon now hired as an investigator by the Public Defender's Office, to collect inside information on the Bramlet case. Gramby had made friends with Robert when the two shared a prison cell.

But first, he and Wendy had to drive back to Nevada to dig up some of Bramlet's clothes.

"Okay, Tom, I'll do whatever you need."

"That's my little Winnerferd," he said and kissed her cheek.

She acted nonchalant but she was terrified. Like Tom, she thought of every move as if it were her last, from the tone of her voice when talking to Tom, to how long and when she should say nothing. Her mind never ignored the nuance of inflection in his voice. The degree of length and curve of his smile gave away genuine happiness or cold calculation. The slightest alteration in the daily routine told her to amplify her awareness, that something had already happened to make him react.

Every word and move in Wendy's life was designed to minimize death. Her own and her child's. A mental chess match that never ended. It was a match of perpetual moves to keep her king alive.

Now here he was about to take an enormous risk by driving into Nevada, likely close to Las Vegas. What if the car broke down? Or someone saw them? It only made sense if his plans were to make himself a widower, if he had resolved to accept that his daughter would grow up as someone else's child.

A bullet behind the ear would make only too much sense. Wendy knew too much. With him in jail and unable to constantly remind her of the wisdom of silence, she could bury him, denying him whatever slim chance he had of getting himself out of this mess. The FBI and police would put the screws to her. They'd use her only weakness, Amy, to break her.

She had to play along. If she voiced her fears outright, he would have killed her right then. "If she's that afraid I'm going to kill her, then she's a risk right now."

A few hours later, they took the highway into Nevada. They drove for hours. Tom wore gloves the entire way. She had never seen him wearing gloves before. It deepened her fears. The entire way, she talked about their life, about their luck in giving birth to such a beautiful, healthy baby, how Amy's face lit up when they both hovered over her. He was a great dad, and the two of them together were even better parents.

Now they were on the road to Pahrump, the faint glimmer of orange and white and red in the sky creating the Strip's electrified version of the Northern Lights.

Tom slowed, turned off the road, and drove on. He slowed to a stop.

"This is it," he said. "Let's go."

He got out of the car, pulled a .22 pistol from his waistband, and pointed her down into a gully.

"Dig right here," he nicked a spot in the soil beneath a bush with the toe of his shoe. "I can't get down there."

The hair stood up on Wendy's arms. Her heart pounded in her temples. It was a cool night but sweat stung her eyes. She found a stick and used it to loosen the soil. Tom stood out of sight, directly behind her. She wanted to turn to face him, but maybe that would make him kill her faster. She still had time.

"I love how Amy smiles when you walk in the room," she said, huffing as she dug. "And when we're with her together, she seems so content, so happy."

She went on and on about the need for a mother and father in a child's life, about how when he got free she and Amy would be waiting. That his gift of a child had made her feel closer to him than ever, made her feel one with him, that no matter what he went through, she was there to help.

Tom stepped closer now, his feet just behind hers.

She stopped talking. Maybe it had backfired. Maybe he thought she was so protective of her baby, she would do anything for the police to ensure the authorities never took Amy.

"Is this good enough?" she asked.

"A little deeper."

She dug a little more. Fast. Frantically.

"There!" she said and jumped up.

His index finger rubbed the barrel of his gun. "Wendy …" he began.

"We should get going, Tom," Wendy interrupted, sure to say 'we.' If we get caught out here, we'd both be in jail tonight."

He pulled something out of the hole. He stuffed the gun

into his pants, turned around, and held back the sharp branches as he led Wendy to the truck.

The twenty-one-year-old mother of a newborn leaned against the door of the car driven by a mob hitman and slept like a baby the last few hours back to Phoenix.

Later, Tom would take Al Bramlet's suit to the dry cleaners in Phoenix and give Wendy the claim ticket.

CHAPTER TWENTY-FIVE

Armed with an arrest warrant detailing the murder of Al Bramlet from the view of Eugene Vaughn, the FBI and a contingent of Las Vegas police headed by Avants arrested Tom and Gramby on April 30, 1977, a Thursday. Newspapers said it happened "without incident." Truth is, Avants would later say, at least two people came very close to being killed.

Avants, his officers, and the FBI moved in on the Phoenix house, with Avants leading the way. They walked up to the house and Gramby emerged—holding a shotgun pointed at Avants.

"He's got the drop on him," Lee thought. But Lee, off to the side, had Gramby in his sights.

"Drop it or I'll blow your fucking head off," Lee ordered.

Avants saw that Lee had "Grams," the police nickname for Gramby, dead to rights. In fact, he wanted Lee to kill him.

"All he ever did was follow his daddy," Avants would later say.

And Avants wanted to kill Tom. He never got the chance. Another detective found Tom first and put him in handcuffs.

Father and son were booked into the Maricopa County jail without a bruise. Bail for each was set at one million dollars on charges of kidnapping and murder. Tom didn't fight extradition to Nevada. But Gramby did. If he could delay transport to Las Vegas long enough, he might be able to get a trial separate from his dad's. Tom's attorneys would have been able to see the shape of the prosecution's case, giving Gramby's attorneys a leg up on formulating a defense.

Or maybe he simply thought escape would be easier in Arizona.

Just after the Fourth of July, Gramby told jailors he was sick. Construction was under way in the jail's infirmary. He climbed some pipes to reach an opening in a wall. His run was short. He was caught quickly and put under escape watch.

"You can't blame me for trying," he told the men who caught him.

Less than two weeks later, Wendy, not yet under arrest for murder, nearly ran down Tom's sister, Jane, with her horse. Wendy was riding by Tom's air conditioning shop. Jane was outside of her house nearby. Wendy trotted up near Jane, not really wanting to hit her but to scare her a bit.

Jane called the police but charges were never filed. "Police say Wendy and the old woman have been fighting over Tom's latest troubles with the law," the *Las Vegas Review-Journal* reported.

It made sense for police to leave Wendy alone. They wanted her on their side in the Bramlet case. They took a long view of the investigation and knew it might take several months of working over Wendy to get her to testify against Tom. To that end, they focused on Robert Peoples, the investigator Tom had entrusted Wendy to.

It wasn't hard to turn Peoples their way. Avants had a talk with him long before the Bramlet murder. He never forgot the story Peoples told of meeting Tom Hanley in the boiler room of Binion's casino. Tom trusted Peoples but began to tell him about all the murders he had committed, perhaps as a way to scare him into never ratting him out.

"You know," Tom concluded, "it seems like every time I meet someone here, someone else dies."

That scared Peoples. So much so that he easily became an informant, a "rat," as Avants called him.

A jury had convicted Peoples of the 1965 murder of Sharon Wilson, shot to death in a room of the El Portal Motel in Beatty, ninety miles north of Las Vegas. Wilson, who worked in a Beatty tavern, the Oasis, signed the motel registration as "Sharon Peoples."

In a room with Peoples and another man while her two children sat outside the door, Wilson died from a bullet that pierced her shoulder, tore through her heart, cracked one vertebrae, and passed out the other side of her body. Peoples testified that Wilson had shot herself, committing suicide. But witnesses in the tavern heard Peoples say he was going to kill her just before they went to the motel. His sentence was life without the possibility of parole.

Peoples' release from prison is a feat that strains the bounds of legal belief given that the man had previously filed numerous appeals with the Nevada and U.S. supreme courts, and finally with the Ninth U.S. Court of Appeals. He failed every time.

Then, somehow, he was released after serving only seven years.

Peoples had a large jaw, crooked smile, and a shock of thick, black hair. He looked like he'd been chiseled from jagged rock. But he had a charm that Wendy was helpless against. He had a high degree of natural intelligence and street smarts cultivated by working since the age of eighteen for the Dragna mob family in Los Angeles. Plus, he was on her side. He made her believe he could set things straight. Truth was, he was firmly in the pocket of homicide chief Avants.

"He says, 'I'll tell you, I can get her out and screw her and get the truth about what happened,'" Avants recalled in a 2005 *Las Vegas Life* article.

Avants snickered. Years later, he would deride Wendy as young and stupid—despite the fact that after Tom's death, she worked on his campaign when he ran for sheriff and nicknamed her the "troubleshooter."

The Hanleys had even tried to get Peoples involved in Bramlet's murder, he confessed. He begged off, telling them he couldn't do it because he never wanted again to face the possibility of returning to prison.

With Tom in jail and orders for her to stick by Peoples' side, Wendy fell for him. Hardened as he was, Peoples fell for Wendy, too. Years later, in a ten-page handwritten summary of that time, he told of his one goal: to keep Wendy alive.

"Wendy would have been dead within two months" if Tom or Gramby somehow had been released from jail before their trials, he wrote. Writing in the third person—so that if anyone ever found the notes, he could say someone else had written them—Peoples wrote that his goal was to see the Hanleys dead.

"Robert had no intentions of keeping the Hanleys in jail—his intent (was to) arrange a contract for their death."

He called his a "strange kind of love" for Wendy, given that he was setting her up to be charged with murder. Then again, he wasn't above committing a crime, with the knowledge of police, to collect information and evidence. He told of one instance where he and a homicide detective waited for a woman, Arlene, to come home. They wanted to question her about some crime. When she got there, they walked into the house with her. She asked to call her lawyer, but they didn't let her. Peoples then "found" some balloons of dope in her handbag, dope that he said he "planted." Faced with a narcotics charge, the woman gave them the information they sought.

Tom so trusted Peoples that when he and Wendy visited for a face-to-face meeting at the jail, where conversations via telephones were recorded, Tom held up a piece of paper to the Plexiglas partition with instructions. They were to dig up Bramlet's sock filled with jewelry and his cowboy boots and underwear, then plant them in Reno to create the impression that Bramlet died there and had never flown back to Las Vegas.

They planned to do it the next day, June 1. That night Wendy and Robert got drunk. He had a room at Ferguson's Motel on Fremont Street. He said, "Why don't we go there?"

Wendy didn't notice when they got there that Peoples simply walked to the front desk and was immediately handed a key. It was to a very specific room, a room right next to another room where homicide detectives wore headphones plugged into a large reel-to-reel tape recorder attached to listening bugs planted in Peoples' room. Everything Peoples and Wendy did or said, they heard and recorded through bugs planted throughout the room.

❖ ❖ ❖

They slept late, then drove to the Ogden Avenue house and got into some grubby clothes—Tom's instructions. He wanted them to look like farmers, he said, as a disguise. Hung over, Wendy flopped into the car and Robert drove as she directed. A caravan of unmarked police cars followed. A small airplane took off from McCarran Airport and followed from high above as they drove west on Blue Diamond Road toward Pahrump.

It took more than two hours to get to the tree that Tom had planted and buried the sock under. The earth was still soft and easy to dig. Robert dug, reached under the root ball, and pulled out the sock that held Al Bramlet's jewelry.

Tom also wanted them to get the boots and underwear. Robert asked Wendy how to get there. She heard the plane overhead and started to panic.

"I don't want to do any more of this," she said. "I just want to go home to my little girl."

"Hey, don't worry about it," Robert assured her. "There's nothing and no one out here but us. Let's just do this and go home."

So she directed him to the bush. Robert got on hands and knees, broke through the loose earth, and pulled out cowboy boots and underwear.

"Okay, let's go. I'll have to get this up to Reno."

They pulled back onto Blue Diamond Road and headed east toward Las Vegas. Wendy dumped the contents of the sock into her lap. Three rings, a money clip, cuff links, a charm, and a necklace.

"Whose jewelry is this?" she asked Robert.

She didn't want to think it was Al's. Tom never told her it was Al's, which allowed her to play the game of denial. She began to cry.

"Don't you know?" Robert asked.

"No, but it looks like Al Bramlet's."

He turned to her, with eyebrows raised and a sarcastic look on his face.

"Come on, you know whose jewelry it is."

"No, I don't!" she said. "But it looks like Al's."

Then Wendy heard something. A small plane was flying low enough to hear its engine. She leaned forward to catch a glimpse through the slanted windshield. Suddenly, a car behind them passed and began to slow down in front of them. Robert slowed, too. Then a car pulled alongside with a portable red emergency light on its hood. Two other cars with those lights followed. The car in front slowed to a stop. Robert was hemmed in by cars on three sides and a sharp dropoff to his right.

"Pull over, this is the police!" ordered an amplified voice from a megaphone affixed to a car.

Robert pulled over. Wendy stuffed the jewelry back into the sock and threw it on Robert's lap.

Suddenly, doors of the car in front flew open, two men got out, and they hunched over with pistols pointed at her and Robert.

Wendy's heart pounded in her temples. "Poor Amy!" she thought. She considered jumping out and down the hillside and running into the desert. Before she could react, a detective walked from the car behind them and opened her door.

A detective stood on the driver's side of the car.

"Do you have any weapons?" he asked Peoples, then ordered him out of the car. As Peoples got out, he grabbed the sock with jewelry inside. Then another detective opened Wendy's door.

"You're under arrest, baby," the detective said.

Handcuffed and inside a squad car, she watched Avants with Peoples. He didn't handcuff him. Just led him to a car and got into the back seat.

After an hour's drive into Las Vegas, they walked into

the homicide office. Wendy was stunned by what she saw: pictures of everyone she knew on a large bulletin board on the wall. Tom's picture was at the top of a pyramid of photos with lines of association drawn between them. Scrawled under Tom's picture were the words "Uncle Tom." An angled line was drawn to a picture of Gramby, who was labeled "Big Headed Kid." Another line connected Tom to a picture of Wendy, labeled "Little Baby."

In handcuffs standing next to Detective Lee, she asked him what "Little Baby" meant.

Lee looked at her with a look so sad, it almost made her cry. "It means you're just a baby playing in a game you know nothing about," he said.

Then Avants walked into his office with Peoples and some other detectives. The lieutenant was smiling. Lee pulled Wendy gently in his direction.

"Come on, baby," he whispered. "It's time to play the game."

CHAPTER TWENTY-SIX

As Tom sat in jail prolonging his day in court while hoping to make a plea deal, Wendy and Robert grew closer.

Tom knew it. His attorney and anyone else with access to him let him know. He never let on that it bothered him. He only talked about his case and Amy, his daughter.

Knowing he would never get out of prison himself, he focused on Gramby. With all the information he and his son had on Las Vegas mobsters, Midwest mobsters, Teamsters, and the Culinary Unions, Tom was certain he could earn at least the chance of freedom someday for his son. Guilt drove him. Agonized him. Why hadn't he done more to help Gramby beat drugs? He talked often to Wendy about somehow getting his son into a monastery, a place of complete solitude where he could pray, save his soul, and spend time creating art. It didn't even have to be a monastery. Hell, let him find a cave on Mount Potosi, just so long as he was alone. Who could he harm if he was left alone?

Wendy had her own battles to fight.

At first, Wendy played tough with investigators. She walked into Avants' office with defiance. For one reason. Tom had killed many people in the past but he'd never been convicted. She had no reason to believe this time would be any different. With that in mind, she could only think about life with Tom out of jail—if she said anything, he'd kill her. If she kept quiet, he'd protect her even more than he already did.

"So, tell us about Bramlet's murder," Avants began.

"I don't know what this is all about," Wendy replied.

"You know exactly what this is about!"

She told him to fuck off and that she wanted to see her lawyer.

Avants had her, though. She had led Peoples to the location of the jewelry. The district attorney charged her with murder, and the court set her bail at $100,000. That was later dropped and Old Man Binion bailed her out after she spent two weeks in jail.

Movement on Tom and Gramby's cases dragged on. Tom's attorney brought up every argument he could think of, from the bias of holding a trial in Las Vegas to illegally obtained evidence. All that summer, police worked on Wendy while searching for a marriage certificate.

Though she had been arrested in early June on a murder charge, chances were slight that a jury would find her guilty of it. Prosecutors and police wanted something on Wendy to use as a lever to ply her for testimony against Tom. So a few weeks later, prosecutors introduced an "accessory to murder" charge. But that charge only stuck if they could prove that she and Tom were not legally married, because Nevada law didn't allow that charge to be leveled against the wife of an accused murderer.

Wendy's attorney argued that they had been married in Montana, and they were searching for the marriage certificate. The deputy district attorney pooh-poohed the idea of the marriage. The court sided with the prosecution and said the two weren't married. The accessory charge stuck, and Wendy briefly went back to jail on $30,000 bail. Benny Binion bailed her out again.

All summer, police pressured Wendy to testify against

Tom. It wasn't difficult. They all saw how she doted on Amy. If she went to prison as a murder accessory, Amy would become a ward of the state, given up for adoption or placed with foster parents who might not give two shits about the her, who'd be happy just to get a monthly check for taking her off the state's hands.

Investigators also knew Tom was seeking a deal. What they needed was more ammunition against him to weaken his position. Feeling they'd already sewn up the Bramlet murder case, they sought information on the bombings.

In October, Wendy was subpoenaed and forced to tell a federal grand jury what she could about two attempted restaurant bombings in January that Tom put into play on behalf of the Culinary Union, which was in a labor battle against both businesses. Police considered the bombings connected to Bramlet's murder—the bombs failed, the story went, so Bramlet never paid the Hanley duo a $10,000 fee. She also testified about what she and Tom did while on the run from authorities and about who called the house after Bramlet disappeared. Wendy also testified that Bramlet owed Tom's air-conditioning business $51,000 for the work he had done for the Culinary Union. Wendy testified the bombs had nothing to do with Bramlet's demise.

Her mom took Amy when Wendy underwent hours of grand jury questioning. She was also allowed to visit Tom while he was in custody. On one of those visits, Tom asked questions and acted concerned about her mom. Wendy's dad had died a few years earlier.

You can't be too careful, Tom advised, shaking his head. Lots of scary people out there these days; never know what might happen in this world.

Wendy took it for what it was, a warning. Keep your

mouth shut, maintain silence, honor the "fence around wisdom."

Because he was in custody, he might not be able to pull the trigger, but he knew many, many people on the outside who could.

In the spring of 1978, Tom and Gramby pleaded guilty to first-degree murder and received life without the possibility of parole. It was called a plea "bargain," because the kidnapping charge was dropped and they would be allowed to serve time in a federal prison vs. one of Nevada's medieval state prisons. Instead of three life sentences, they got only one. Father and son, although both imprisoned, were placed in the Federal Witness Protection program.

The life sentences were mandatory in Nevada. But a prosecutor in the case said it was too bad he couldn't give Tom the death penalty, "because he sure deserves it."

Of course, Tom expected more freedom in the future. The two had information the Feds wanted. They could answer questions. Who hired them to do the bombings? What was the real reason behind Bramlet's killing? How deeply was the union tied to the mob? Unions in general had mob ties, but how far and high did it go?

Charging the two for the restaurant and tavern bombings in Las Vegas was secondary to the Feds, is how Avants saw it. He went to them with the information Wendy had revealed about Tom and Gramby's part in the bombings. They took the information, smiled, and, in essence, closed the door. They didn't want to convict the Hanleys, they wanted to use them to testify about what they knew about the unions and its ties to the mob.

"We didn't have a very close relationship with the Feds at that time," Avants said more than thirty years later at his home in Las Vegas. "There were some strained relationships there, because they would withhold this story and that story, but when they came to us, we laid out everything for them. They just wouldn't return the favor."

After Tom and Gramby's conviction, they were treated to a tour of select cities around the United States. Milwaukee. Chicago. Kansas City. Washington, D.C. At each stop, in super-secret hearings behind closed doors, they each spilled what they knew about the Teamsters' and Culinary Union's ties to the International Culinary Union—which many saw as the money behind the bullets in Bramlet's body—the Outfit, the Syndicate, and other organized crime operations in the United States.

At night, Tom called Wendy. He could only tell her what city he was in, tell her it was "more grand jury stuff," then ask about his daughter and any Las Vegas news.

Wendy had some news. The Feds had offered to hide her in the Witness Protection Program as well. Their rationale was that she knew too much about Tom and Gramby's criminal activities—who they talked to, who called their house, and all the people Tom claimed to have killed, and for whom. Meanwhile, Tom and Gramby were on "grand jury" tour, which meant someone might send them a message by trying to kill Wendy or Amy. So the offer was made: She and Amy could go into the program, hidden forever from her mom or anyone else she knew.

She refused.

Then she was almost killed.

In March 1978, Wendy pleaded guilty to the gross misdemeanor of conspiracy to prevent the due administration of law. All the murder charges had been dropped. Wendy spoke up in court, alleging she had been brainwashed by

Tom and Gramby, "good con artists." The judge gave her one year of probation.

Two months later, in May, she was driving on Valley View Boulevard when the car in front of her signaled a left turn. She began to turn right to go around him. She told police a car to her right hemmed her in, so she had no choice but to hit the truck in front of her. Then she spun into the oncoming lane of traffic and hit another car. Newspaper accounts differed, however. Police told reporters she was driving too fast and couldn't swerve around the car in front of her fast enough, then hit it and spun into oncoming traffic.

Whichever case it was, the driver of the third car, Robert Brandt, was transported to Valley Hospital with minor injuries.

An ambulance took her to Desert Springs Hospital, where a group of police officers and homicide detectives awaited. They feared the accident was no accident. Another attempt might be coming. So they secretly sent her to another hospital. Then rushed her to a third hospital the next day.

None of that was reported. In November 1981, Brandt's body was found in the trunk of his own car on the side of a desert road outside of Las Vegas. No arrests were ever made.

CHAPTER TWENTY-SEVEN

In April 1979, Tom and Gramby pleaded guilty to constructing and planting bombs in three Las Vegas non-union restaurants. U.S. District Judge Harry Claiborne, who had once represented Tom when he was charged with killing Ralph Alsup, and was considered by Wendy to be a close family friend, sentenced them to an additional five years to run at the same time as their current prison term.

The news meant little to Wendy, who was still grieving the death of her mother from an aneurysm a month earlier. She and Peoples were married. Peoples is the man Amy came to know as "Dad."

In October of that year, Judge Claiborne ordered Tom to undergo a competency exam after defense attorney Oscar Goodman questioned his mental status. Goodman represented Ben Schmoutey, who filled in as Culinary Union chief after Bramlet's death and was by this time charged as being part of the Las Vegas restaurant bombings.

A month later, Tom died at Valley Hospital of "natural causes." At his funeral a week later, only a handful of people showed up. Wendy wasn't among them. Neither was Gramby, who wasn't allowed out of prison to attend.

Wendy's marriage to Robert Peoples lasted a decade. Wendy then took Amy and moved moved to Reno. There she met a local television weatherman and became a political fundraiser. She worked on several major campaigns, including those for governor, congressman, mayor, district attorney, and city council.

Later, Wendy opened a car dealership. Her childhood best friend and brother, Michael, stole cars from the lot after she helped get him released from prison. He went back to prison. He's serving time in Oregon today.

Eventually, the relationship with the weatherman folded, but not before Wendy had another daughter, Robin, in 1990.

There were other adventures. In 2010, a Las Vegas television station did a report based on a sworn deposition in which Wendy alleged that during the '90s, she had lived for six months with a woman who was the mistress of Jim Gibbons, a married man who had served in the Nevada Legislature. Gibbons became a U.S. congressman in 1997 until he was elected Nevada's governor in 2006. Wendy did more than simply allege that Gibbons was having an affair. She and Gibbons' mistress, she asserted, took frequent trips to California. There they picked up cash, on at least a few occasions, then drove back to Reno. On one occasion, she said, she watched the mistress hand the money to Gibbons.

Gibbons denied all of Wendy's allegations, saying that at the time of the alleged money collections he wasn't even in elected office so why would he be getting cash? He also denied having a mistress.

She and Amy moved back to Las Vegas. Around the turn of the century, she met another man, Carl Mazaros, a prop master for Hollywood movies who had moved to Las Vegas and worked on productions in Strip resorts. They married in 2005.

Outwardly, life slowed for Wendy. To a nice, predictable, comfortable pace. Inside?

In 2005, she was on a cell phone talking to a writer for *Las Vegas Life* magazine. In his article, the writer recounted what happened next, when Wendy stopped talking while describing how happy she was to have gotten through it all and survived.

"She stops mid-sentence and her breathing over the phone becomes heavier. 'Hold on,' she says. 'The sheriff just pulled up.'

"And now she's panting because she's running into the house.

"'There's a cop outside!' she tells someone as the sound of a door slamming can be heard. 'He's right outside! I left my purse out there on the sidewalk.'

"Moments later, she learns that it's just a constable dropping off the medical bills of a relative who lives across the street. ... She bursts into fitful, nervous laughter.

"'It's a medical bill, just a medical bill!' she says, and she's still laughing. 'Did you hear how scared I got? Did you hear?'"

EPILOGUE

George Knapp had the same visceral reaction to Wendy's stories as many who read this book will have: interest tinged with a healthy dose of skepticism.

Even a longtime, award-winning television journalist can go an entire career without hearing a story like this: a father-son hitman team that may have been the most prolific contract killers in the United States. Not only that, but when Knapp started to uncover more information, he realized the story of the Hanleys had been largely forgotten since the '70s.

So he did what good journalists do. He dug. Asked questions. He shakes his head and smiles now at what he found. He's still a bit astonished.

"So much of what she said is consistent with what these lawmen I had interviewed were saying," Knapp says. "The fact is, you had a father-son hitman team. And the fact that they were so prolific, even if you limited it to the ones they did in the Southwest."

He described first eliciting information from Wendy as akin to "pulling teeth."

"Some points she wouldn't go beyond," Knapp says. "She was still afraid they would come after her. And I don't think that's entirely unfounded. She was someone who lived with very prolific killers for a lot of years and was in a position to know a lot of stuff. She was the kind of person that some probably didn't want around anymore."

Knapp's interviews with Wendy, law enforcement officials, and others culminated in an hour-long television special in 2000 for the television station (KLAS-TV Channel 8) where he heads a team of investigative reporters.

The show includes an interview with Las Vegas homicide detective David Hatch, now retired. Described by Knapp as "one of the best" homicide detectives he's ever known, Hatch pulled no punches about the scope of Tom and Gramby Hanley's deadly endeavors.

"They were probably two of the most active contract murderers in the Western states," Hatch said, adding that after reviewing cold cases from 1943 to 1982, Tom and Gramby were linked to seven homicides.

"In our jurisdiction, in at least seven they are the dominant suspects in all of them," Hatch says. "I think between here and Phoenix, I know they did stuff down there. I don't think this (seven) is a third of who they killed. I really don't. These people were total, cold-blooded killers."

The more Knapp talked to Wendy, the more she relaxed and opened up. During interviews for this book, she would have moments when memories buried for years bubbled to the surface and poured out.

"I think she pushed those memories deep down, and that makes a lot of sense to me," Knapp says. "She's been frightened the whole time I've known her, and with good reason. Gramby's still alive, and she dealt with some bad people, some of whom are still around. I think Tom Hanley scared the shit out of her. And Tom was a scary person. Gramby was a scary person. So much was said to her to scare her, to keep a handle on her, to scare her into control. 'Silence is the fence around wisdom.' That can really mess with someone's head."

After his TV special aired, federal and local law enforcement began to show up and ask Wendy questions.

"All of them found Wendy credible within limits," Knapp says. "All of them considered her to be a worthy witness, a potential case-breaking witness. Of course, if you're trying to nail down enough information to get an indictment or to pin a murder on someone to be a worthy witness, Wendy alone wasn't enough."

One of the most unnerving moments in the documentary comes during an interview with Robert Peoples, the same man who double-crossed Wendy but then married her for ten years. Peoples, who died a few years ago, looks into the camera. He says that back in the late '70s he was under contract, presumably by the mob, to kill Tom Hanley to keep him from talking after he was arrested for Al Bramlet's murder.

Then he says something about Tom Hanley that chills.

"He had just one fault," Peoples said. "He had to kill. He did like a person had to eat. He had to kill."

The Twisted Tale of a Vegas Rag Doll

My first love was Innocence.
Tainted memories I share in repentance.
The price of my pride was self-existence.
Comfort became my only resistance.

My second love was Purity.
Survival murdered my virginity.
Tears stole the years of serenity.
I became their trophy for identity.

My third love was Aspiration.
Their shadows followed me in accusation.
Rape, murder and extortion were their operation.
I became an act of desperation.

My fourth love was Confusion.
Their social lies were an illusion.
Tomorrow I'll write their conclusion.
I became hypnotized by their spell of delusion.

My fifth love was Unity.
I refused the Witness Protection immunity.
Silence is the fence around wisdom's gratuity.
This fight became a light of opportunity.

My sixth love was Redemption.
My life was marked; so I settled in deception.
Fear and disgrace were no exception.
Comfort became my only temptation.

My seventh love was Fate.
Never again will I climb into their cage.
My daughters gave me the courage to escape.
I became empowered before it was too late.

My eighth love was Hope.
Dismantling their empire; to see it up in smoke.
They will be humiliated in the shackles they gloat.
I became the warrior they thought they broke.

My ninth love was Survival.
Into the future is my arrival.
God was my shield and love was my rifle.
I became the soldier of my soul for revival.

My tenth love is Everything in-between.
Into the eyes of the Devil, I have seen.
I just want my soul to be clean.
I'm taking back the woman I wanted to be.

—*J. R. Farrell*

ACKNOWLEDGMENTS

Joe Schoenmann: Not to get philosophical, but it is nearly impossible to thank all the people who help a writer in the creation of a book. Thanks need to go not just to those who helped in the research, endured interviews, took the time to read passages, or didn't even realize they were helping simply by talking about the book. Appreciation also goes to those who listened patiently to complaints about just how damned difficult it is to write a book. Yes, I whined.

Those who helped include Las Vegas' two daily newspapers, the *Las Vegas Sun*, which allowed me to use several weeks of vacation time over a few short months to work on this book; and the *Las Vegas Review-Journal*, which let down its competitive guard long enough to let me—a reporter for the competition—rummage through its newspaper morgue.

Then, in no particular order: Geoff Schumacher, Carolyn Hayes Uber, Peter Schoenmann, Jan Schoenmann, Michael Squires, Scott Dickensheets, George Knapp, Ruth Miller, Marlene Greenfield, Sandy Ducharme, Lynn Foster, Michelle Leifer, Susie McCormick, Amairani Hernandez, Jaq Greenspon, Starbucks on Maryland Parkway, The Beat on Fremont Street, Lied Library on the UNLV campus, Todd Korgan, Kate Hausbeck, Jonah Schoenmann, Rebecca Clifford Cruz, Tom Gorman, and, of course, Wendy.

Wendy Mazaros: A very special thank you to my co-author Joe Schoenmann, whose admirable writing skills coupled with patience and understanding, often required reading my mind and heart which was not an easy task. Also thanks to my editor Geoff Schumacher for his meticulous eye and hard work. Most of all, gratitude to my publisher, Carolyn Hayes Uber, for giving me the opportunity to tell my story. I appreciate all her contributions of time and ideas, as she guided us through the book process and the funding to make this book a reality.

I thank my family for their unconditional love: To my dear husband Carl, for being the most understanding, loving, caring, patient, supportive husband throughout the progress of this book, as it became a reality. I'm so blessed to have found someone who loves me, past and all. Amy, my darling daughter, if you were not born, I would never have had the strength to continue in this world. You, my dear, helped me through the most difficult time of my life. Robin, you are the most precious daughter a mother could ask for. You encouraged me with positive thoughts while I worked on this book. Your spirit and heart are generous and beautiful. You and your sister Amy are my link to life and love. I'm grateful to my grandbabies, Dylan, Danny and Devin for having so much patience with Nana while she was creating her memoir. This book is for you my darlings, knowing one day when you grow up and read this book, you will know and understand the cycle of evil turned good. You, my dear grandbabies, will prove to the world, evil can be conquered, because you will be living proof.

I owe a debt of gratitude to my friends, I salute and thank my oldest and dearest friend Mylan Hawkins, for her loyalty as a true friend, through the years, Mylan never once gave up on me. Mylan, you are my rock. A big thank you to all of my Facebook friends online, whom expressed so much excitement, enthusiasm, and encouragement. It makes me grateful and humbled at the same time. Bless you all.